If . . . Then . . . Curriculum: Assessment-Based Instruction, Grade 4

Lucy Calkins with Colleagues from the Teachers College Reading and Writing Project

Photography by Peter Cunningham

HEINEMANN ◆ PORTSMOUTH, NH

W9-CCD-862

*first*hand
An imprint of Heinemann
361 Hanover Street
Portsmouth, NH 03801–3912
www.heinemann.com

Offices and agents throughout the world

© 2013 by Lucy Calkins

All rights reserved. No part of this book may be reproduced in any form or by any electronic or mechanical means, including information storage and retrieval systems, without permission in writing from the publisher, except by a reviewer, who may quote brief passages in a review, with the exception of reproducible pages, which are identified by the *Units of Study in Opinion, Information, and Narrative Writing* copyright line and can be photocopied for classroom use only.

"Dedicated to Teachers" is a trademark of Greenwood Publishing Group, Inc.

The authors and publisher wish to thank those who have generously given permission to reprint borrowed material:

Quote by Roald Dahl. Used by permission of David Higham Associates.

Cataloging-in-Publication data is on file with the Library of Congress.

ISBN-13: 978-0-325-04814-7
ISBN-10: 0-325-04814-2

Production: Elizabeth Valway, David Stirling, and Abigail Heim
Cover and interior designs: Jenny Jensen Greenleaf
Series includes photographs by Peter Cunningham, Nadine Baldasare, and Elizabeth Dunford
Composition: Publishers' Design and Production Services, Inc.
Manufacturing: Steve Bernier

Printed in the United States of America on acid-free paper
17 16 15 14 13 VP   3 4 5

Contents

PART TWO: Differentiating Instruction for Individuals and Small Groups: If . . . Then . . . Conferring Scenarios

Introduction

FOURTH GRADE IS A CRUCIAL YEAR, a turning point of sorts. Howard Gardner has described the final preteen years as a "sensitive period" during which skills must be developed at a rapid rate so that by the time students reach their teens, they are accomplished enough to withstand the rise in their own critical powers (*Art, Mind, and Brain*, 1984, 90). But Gardner also feels that in these upper elementary years, children are supremely equipped to learn just about anything. He quotes V. S. Pritchart's reference to this as "the eager period" (*The Cab at the Door*, 1968, 102). Gardner writes, "If one has any doubts about the particular learning facility of this period, one should travel to a foreign country with a preadolescent and note who picks up the language and without a trace of accent" (214).

Fourth-graders are poised to grow in important ways as writers. They are ready to internalize writing strategies so that what are, at first, concrete, methodical procedures become far more fleeting, flexible, and efficient ways of working. Instead of writing out four leads to a text and then progressing through an intricate system of voting on those leads, fourth-graders who have already done this sort of work in a concrete, hands-on fashion are able to mull over possible leads in their minds, jotting onto the page only those options that feel particularly worth considering.

With these new abilities comes new resolve to excel. By the time they are in fourth grade, some students have begun to worry about doing well. Some are aware of high-stakes tests and fret over the impending judgments. Fourth-graders are on the brink of adolescence but not yet there; it is a precious year.

In this series, we see fourth grade as a powerful opportunity. We believe that most students at this point can begin to learn the expectations of academic writing. While we could have helped them fend off academic pressures for as long as possible, showing fourth-graders small ways to ramp up their third-grade work so that it (barely) meets expectations for fourth grade, we've done the opposite. We've embraced the challenge of bringing fourth-graders into the rigors of academic writing. We teach youngsters to write thesis-driven essays that are for the most part very similar to the essays, they'll write on their SAT exams. They use the essay structure to write thesis-driven literary essays, too, including compare-and-contrast essays. We dive deep into the challenges of research reports, showing them how to delve into primary sources, cite their sources, and work toward logically structuring their research reports.

But here's the thing. We know fourth-graders very, very well, and we use that knowledge to do everything we can to provide these youngsters with step-by-step instruction that leads to increased proficiency. We don't assume, but instead spell things out. We anticipate that youngsters will first produce fairly simple versions of academic writing, and we show them how to take those early efforts and improve them. So, for instance, fourth-graders' first experience writing thesis-driven essays occurs in a spirited boot camp in which the whole class works together to compose an essay in defense of ice cream. Only after youngsters have internalized the simplest possible version of a "boxes-and-bullets" essay do we show them optional structures and more complex alternatives. In a similar way, the process of learning to elaborate on sections of a report is broken down to a granular level. Children are taught that within a report—say, on the American Revolution—they can embed small narratives such as those one might write in a "day in the life of . . ." piece. Within that same research report, students can also embed essays (such as an essay claiming that the Boston Tea Party played a big role in the Revolutionary War).

One of the ways fourth-graders are brought along to new heights is through a careful attention to transferring what they learned while working in one kind of writing to their work with other kinds of writing. In *The Arc of Story: Writing Realistic Fiction*, fourth-graders learn new ways to link one scene together with another scene. This knowledge becomes foundational to later work with transitions in *Boxes and Bullets: Personal and Persuasive Essays* and in *The Literary Essay: Writing about Fiction.*

The fourth-grade books, then, create an indispensable curriculum that provides students with the foundation they need before they move to the rigors of fifth-grade and middle school writing. Because the fourth-grade curriculum is essential, it is important to assess your students, review the *Units of Study* books, and decide the best sequence in which to present the units. You will no doubt find that you want to supplement the curriculum in the four *Units of Study* books. The upcoming section will help you make plans to do that work, based on your students' needs and abilities.

IF . . . THEN . . . : ASSESSMENT-BASED PLANNING

The fourth-grade units were devised with the expectation that children enter fourth grade having already studied the meat-and-potatoes of narration, information, and opinion writing, with many children presumably studying these within the units that are captured in the third-grade books—*Crafting True Stories, The Art of Information Writing,* and *Changing the World: Persuasive Speeches, Petitions, and Editorials.* (*Once Upon a Time* is a favorite third-grade unit but less essential as a foundation for fourth grade.) There are, of course, other ways for children to have developed enough basic skills in writing that they enter your classroom poised to make great strides in the fourth-grade units we've provided.

However, there may be some instances when you decide that it is best to not plunge children immediately into *The Arc of Story* or another one of the fourth-grade books.

If you start the year with a performance assessment, this will reveal a bit about the level at which your children are writing, and you can use this information to plan your year. We find that at the start of the school year, youngsters are rusty from the summer, so before you conduct the assessment, you probably want to show children some writing that other fourth-graders have written, asking them to tell you what they notice the author has done, and perhaps you'll want to give them a chance to write in their notebooks for a bit, just to reacquaint themselves with writers. This can give you a quick sense of the goals they are accustomed to working toward and the language they use for talking about those goals. Meanwhile, this inquiry reminds children who enter fourth grade with a background in writing to use what they know.

After two or three days or so in which you immerse your children in narrative writing, you'll ask them to take fifty minutes and write the best personal narrative they can write. You may want to make this on-demand writing feel celebratory—give your students a chance to show off what they know about narrative writing. You might say, "I'm really eager to understand what you can do as writers, so before you do anything else, please spend today writing the very best personal narrative, the best Small Moment story, of one particular time in your life. You'll have fifty minutes to write this true story of one small moment. Write in a way that shows me all that you know about how to do this kind of writing." You may also want to spell out some of your expectations for narrative writing—see the prompt we provide in *Writing Pathways: Performance Assessments and Learning Progressions, K–5.* While the students are writing, be sure you don't coach them. Don't remind them to write with details or to focus. You want to see what they do in a hands-off situation—and frankly, you want to be in a position to show great growth from this starting point. That means you'll really want to find out what their starting points are, so you can extend their skills. The data you collect by doing an on-demand writing assessment will be invaluable as you take the time to learn what your students already know and can do.

When you sit with the writing texts they produce, brace yourself!

The first thing to keep in mind is that the fourth-grade expectations are for the far end of the school year (and frankly, they are not necessarily expectations for a fifty-minute on-demand writing time, anyhow). You are absolutely *not* expecting children to enter fourth grade producing on-demand writing that is at the fourth-grade level. You should feel very pleased if many of your children are somewhere in the ballpark of writing at the third-grade level (because that means they haven't had summer slippage and are starting fourth grade just about where they should be). If your children are writing narratives that are in the midway range between second and third grade, they are well positioned to participate in the fourth-grade units. On the other hand, if some of their narratives are at the first-grade level, and many others at the second-grade level, you'll need to plan to teach forcefully this year, but you should still be able to accomplish the job. What do you do in that instance?

You have two options. You might decide to postpone the first unit in the series, *The Arc of Story,* and first teach the precursor unit, "Raising the Level of Personal Narrative Writing." Your children would then enter the fiction unit in strong stead. Alternatively, you could plunge into the fiction unit, making a small detour fairly early on to help students with the most critical piece—learning to write scenes, not summaries (which can also be described as learning to story-tell, not summarize).

The situation with information writing will not be all that different. That is, the fourth-grade series expects that students have had experience writing all-about information texts. The unit *Bringing History to Life* begins in an accessible way, and all children should feel comfortable at the start, but by the third bend, children are tasked to do some very challenging work. If your students have strong literacy skills and an aptitude for challenge, even if they enter this unit appearing to write at the second-grade level in on-demand assessment (of course, you hope this is not the case), they will relish this unit. But if the children are struggling readers and writers, are easily overwhelmed, and did not come from a third-grade classroom in which these units were taught, you will almost certainly want to teach a precursor unit in information writing and to let them do that kind of writing first. "Informational Writing: Writing about Topics of Personal Expertise" lets children learn to write reports about topics they know well and teaches within that context the essential structures in information writing. This provides a great foundation before students move to topics that require research. Alternatively, you could borrow the third-grade book, *The Art of Information Writing*, and teach that unit before *Bringing History to Life*.

If you find your children need added support in informational writing, chances are good they will need the same in essay writing. In this instance, we do not recommend you take on a detour unit. Instead, we recommend you begin with the book *Boxes and Bullets: Personal and Persuasive Essays*. This will set children well on their way toward writing cohesive, well-structured, and persuasive essays. The next challenge will be teaching them to transfer these skills to writing essays *about texts*. The book *The Literary Essay: Writing about Fiction* is a challenging and important one. If you have the time to do so, you might teach a simpler unit on writing about reading first. This simpler unit is described in this book: "The Literary Essay: Equipping Ourselves with the Tools to Write Expository Texts that Advance an Idea about Literature."

All of the units we have described so far focus on a kind of writing, and it is also wonderful to teach units that focus on portions of the process of writing. The "Revision" unit in this book gives writers the opportunity to revisit and rewrite old pieces of writing to gain practice lifting the level of their earlier work. Revision can be a hard sell for writers of all ages yet proves again and again to be one of the most powerful tools writers possess. This unit will go a long way toward helping your young writers jump on the revision bandwagon!

This book will also help students at the other end of the spectrum who enter your class as proficient writers, breezing through the main units of study and acting ready for more learning! For these students—all your students, really—we offer several supplemental units. "Historical Fiction: Teaching Complex Texts" is an advanced fiction writing unit that follows up on the work in *The Arc of Story* and helps children develop the means and know-how to transfer and apply all they've learned about narrative craft. Children will jump at the opportunity to write in this genre, and repeated practice in narrative writing will move your writers closer and closer to the ambitious Common Core narrative standards for fourth and fifth grades. This unit is a great favorite, and of course, it works especially well if children are reading as well as writing historical fiction.

Those who are concerned about readying students for the CCSS' emphasis on close reading of complex texts will probably want to reserve a month for a unit of study on writing poetry. "Poetry Anthologies: Writing, Thinking, and Seeing More" ushers children into a study that supports connections between reading and writing and teaches writers to zoom in on craft and its relation to meaning. In this unit, children play with language and study mentor texts as they learn to use poetry to convey specific themes and messages.

And finally, "Journalism" is an old favorite, a unit in which students develop the ability to write concisely, clearly, and with purposeful organization. It won't be long before your fourth-graders are running around, writing notebook in hand, looking for the next great lead for an article!

Part One: Alternate and Additional Units

Raising the Level of Personal Narrative Writing

RATIONALE/INTRODUCTION

Although the Units of Study volume *The Arc of Story: Writing Realistic Fiction* is designed to launch the year, you may feel your children aren't yet ready to do that work. Perhaps they still struggle with writing a focused, cohesive piece, and you want to spend a bit longer teaching the essentials of narrative writing and the structure of a small moment. Then too, *you* might feel tied to personal narrative and want to start your year with a unit that invites youngsters to bring their lives into the classroom.

Right from the start, one of your priorities will be to teach writing in such a way that students write a tremendous amount, and a unit in personal narrative writing encourages this. Students simply can't get better at writing without writing—and in this unit students do lots of writing. Perhaps just as important, the ability to craft a good narrative is especially valuable because it is a transferable skill; narratives underlie or are embedded within almost any other genre. What makes an essay have a great deal of persuasive power but the presence of poignant anecdotes and vignettes—that is, powerful personal narratives? Pay attention to journalism, speeches, and compelling expository texts, and you'll notice the power of embedded anecdotes. The importance of narrative writing is such that the Common Core State Standards and the National Assessment for Educational Progress both suggest that 35 percent of the writing that fourth-graders do across the entire day (including the time spent writing within the content areas and in response to reading) should be narratives. Students will find it easier to meet the expectations of the Common Core and of other formal educational measures when they have opportunities for substantial practice, feedback, and instruction in narrative writing.

Finally, and perhaps above all, thirty years of work in writing classrooms have shown us that there is no better way to create a community of trust, which is fundamental to producing good writing, than to tell children that their stories—their lives—are worth recording. When children feel safe with their peers, when they are inspired to write because they believe they have meaningful stories to tell, when they learn the skills and strategies that published authors use to great effect, then they will be eager to write and write well.

In this unit, you'll strive toward two goals—increased independence and dramatic growth in the level of your students' writing. Right from the start, then, you'll want to convey to students the expectation that both their writing and their autonomy will improve and grow in obvious, dramatic ways with each new unit of study. These two goals are interrelated, and you will organize your writing workshop so that students work with great investment toward clear goals, choosing from a repertoire of strategies. Both the Common Core State Standards and Webb's Depth of Knowledge levels call for students to work with progressive independence and increasing levels of cognitive demand. Those goals are within your grasp.

MANDATES, TESTS, STANDARDS

This unit, combined with *The Arc of Story: Writing Realistic Fiction*, will enable your students to meet the expectations of the Common Core State Standards for narrative writing, which are extremely ambitious. For example, the fourth-grade sample text in Appendix B of the CCSS begins like this:

Glowing Shoes

One quiet, Tuesday morning, I woke up to a pair of bright, dazzling shoes, lying right in front of my bedroom door. The shoes were a nice shade of violet and smelled like catnip. I found that out because my cats, Tigger and Max, were rubbing on my legs, which tickled.

When I started out the door, I noticed that Tigger and Max were following me to school. Other cats joined in as well. They didn't even stop when we reached Main Street!

"Don't you guys have somewhere to be?" I quizzed the cats.

"Meeeeeeooooow!" the crowd of cats replied.

As I walked on, I observed many more cats joining the stalking crowd. I moved more swiftly. The crowd of cats' walk turned into a prance. I sped up. I felt like a roller coaster zooming past the crowded line that was waiting for their turn as I darted down the sidewalk with dashing cats on my tail.

It's easy to see that this fourth-grade writer has fluency with narrative craft. The way the characters (both human and animal) converse, the attention to tiny details, the small actions that layer one on another to build story tension—these are the marks of a young writer who knows something about narrative writing. It takes a great deal of instruction and practice to build this prowess.

Because the skills your students develop while working in one genre of writing can be transferred and applied to other genres, it will be especially important that you are mindful of the overarching ways in which the CCSS raise the ante for fourth-grade narrative writers. For example, the standards ask writers to consider audience more than ever before. Children are to "orient" readers, "manage the sequence of events," and use words and details to "convey experiences and events precisely."

ASSESSMENT, RUBRICS, AND CALIBRATING INSTRUCTION

You want your students to write with independence and stamina, and an important aspect of that is for their writing to become dramatically better during the unit.

After children have written on-demand narratives, you will probably want to talk about that writing. You may decide to collect some of the qualities of good writing that you saw many students were able to put into action. You might ask students to do some self-evaluation, analyzing their own writing for evidence of those qualities that you saw. You may want to give children an opportunity to show their on-demand writing to a partner, citing evidence of what they did as writers. Within a few days of being back in school, your students should be acting, thinking, and talking like writers.

Your job is not only to give this on-demand assessment but also to take seriously the challenge of making sure that as the unit unfolds, your instruction is calibrated around this data, and the students' work gets progressively better. The on-demand writing can function as your starting gate. After students collect narrative entries for a few more days, you will want to ask them to look back at their on-demand piece and at the narrative entries they have written since then. Are the entries they have written since the start of school dramatically better than their on-demand pieces? Frankly, all too often we have seen students' writing go downhill, as if they tried hard on the first day, when being assessed, and then just dutifully filled the page every day after that. If students' work is not improving in palpable ways, you will want to act shocked and say, "This simply can't be! Go back and rewrite this entry, making it your very best."

John Hattie, in *Visible Learning* (2008), compiled thousands of studies from every walk of life that attempt to understand the factors that support achievement. Looking at data from twenty to thirty million students to identify factors that were especially influential, Hattie came away saying that it is incredibly important for learners to be working toward crystal-clear, challenging, but accessible, goals and for them to receive informative feedback that specifies what is working and clarifies the next steps they can take. It will be important, then, for you to illuminate for students what it is that they are trying to accomplish.

Early in this unit, you'll give students the opportunity to study examples of what they are aiming to create. Help them engage in close reading of mentor texts that will illustrate narrative craft that you believe is accessible for your students. Then, too, give children opportunities to look between the texts they've written and those they aim to write, thinking, "What's the work I'm going to do next?" They may even create a personal goal sheet on which they record the strategy or goal they are working on. And certainly, you'll want to give them ample time to study the rubrics you use to assess them.

The act of setting goals for themselves is important for writers, making it likely that they will not just be filling up pages in a writer's notebook but will consciously work toward qualities of good writing they admire in the mentor texts.

You will also want to set children up to work toward the Narrative Writing Checklist that is within reach for them. If you are teaching this unit rather than plunging students directly into *The Art of Story*, it may be that your students aren't yet working toward the fourth-grade narrative checklist. That's okay—but they will need to work with special resolve and urgency toward whatever goals *are* within their reach. Expect that progress can take a week, not a month!

A SUMMARY OF THE BENDS IN THE ROAD FOR THIS UNIT

In Bend I (Generate Lots of Narrative Writing), children will study samples of the kind of writing they hope to create—personal narratives—paying close attention to what makes these so successful. They will recall strategies they may have learned in years past and learn new strategies for uncovering life moments that are especially significant. Throughout the first bend, children will lift the level of volume and stamina in their writing. Finally, they will be reminded that writing is not just about creating text but about writing *well*. Even before beginning their first drafts, children will assess their entries against the narrative checklist, select goals for themselves, and learn strategies for lifting the level of the writing.

In Bend II (Select a First Seed Idea and Take a Piece through the Writing Process), students will choose a seed idea to develop and will then progress through the process of writing, drawing on strategies they learned in prior personal narrative units and ones they learn during this unit. They'll use timelines to try out different ways their stories might go, and will try storytelling their draft one way, then another. They'll ask themselves, "What do I want my reader to know and feel?" They'll experiment, especially with beginning and ending their pieces at different points in the story. They will learn a variety of strategies for editing. At the end of the bend, children will set this first piece aside and prepare to go through the writing process a second time with a new topic, a new seed idea.

In Bend III (Transference and Application: Go through the Writing Process Again with Greater Independence), students will choose a new seed idea, rehearse, and then fast-draft again. They will learn more complex, nuanced ways to revise, focusing not only on writing vividly and revealing the external and internal stories but also on conveying what their story is *really* about. Children will learn to be the boss of their own writing life: self-assessing, setting goals, and bringing all they've learned to bear on this new piece of writing. They will learn that the end goal is not just to make better writing but to get better as a *writer*. At the end of the bend, students will choose between their first and second draft, picking one to bring to final publication.

GETTING READY
Establish Routines and Structures

As you institute routines and structures that will set children up to work with engagement and some independence, think about the background your students bring; if there are systems from the previous year that can be reinvigorated, that will allow you to get you started quickly. Of course, you'll want to establish your own rituals as well as reinvigorating ones that may have worked in previous years. What will the system be for homework? What will your system be for collecting and reading student work? Will you collect the work from one table of writers every Monday and another table every Tuesday? Will you devote one evening a week to reviewing all student work? Will partners sit beside each other in the meeting area and also at their work areas, or will you ask partners to choose a meeting space—sometimes, for those who can handle it, on the floor? Where will paper be kept, and what system will ensure that students have access to supplies without coming to you?

Most fourth-grade teachers expect that students keep their writing notebooks with them, carrying them between home and school every day, unless you ask to review them. If a writer leaves his or her notebook at home, convey with urgency, "Could we call someone at your house and get it here?" If you treat this in a ho-hum way, half your class will leave their notebooks at home. Expect your students to proceed in order through their writer's notebook, not skipping pages helter-skelter. You may want students to date each day's work and record H (for home) or S (for school), so that together you can study their productivity in each place. Fourth-grade teachers generally expect about an equal amount of work to be done at home and at school, and hope students write a page and a half a day at the start of the year. Obviously some students will not write that much yet, and this will be especially true if students weren't in writing workshops during previous years.

You'll channel these kids to produce more: "Keep your hand moving." "Writers should be writing." "Ten more minutes. In that time, you've got to get to the bottom of the page." "That's it, you wrote a *lot* more than you were writing last week. Nice progress. Now see if you can get onto the second page. That can be your new goal, okay?"

Gather Texts

As children learn about narrative writing, some of the lessons will be *explicit*, taught in minilessons and conferences, and some of the lessons will be *implicit*, gleaned as children study texts that sound like the ones they will soon write. Even just one dearly loved and closely studied text can infuse a writing workshop with new energy and lots of opportunities for implicit learning. Plan to read a few focused narratives aloud and to pull your students close to study one or two with tremendous detail. Be sure the mentor texts you use in this unit are not ones students have studied previously. We recommend you consider Brinkloe's *Fireflies!*; "Eating the World" or "Statue," from Ralph Fletcher's memoir *Marshfield Dreams*; "Mr. Entwhistle," from Jean Little's *Hey World, Here I Am!*; *Those Shoes*, by Maribeth Boelts. If your class is especially advanced, you might study "Everything Will Be Okay," by James Howe; selections from Amy Erlich's *When I Was Your Age: Original Stories About Growing Up*; excerpts from Jean Little's memoir *Little by Little*; or John Coy's *Strong to the Hoop*.

If you cannot comfortably assume the role of writing mentor in your class, it will be all the more crucial that you read aloud texts written by other authors and tell stories of the authors' writing lives and identities. You might also read aloud texts that talk about writing and the writing life. We recommend, for example,

Reynolds's little picture book *Ish*; Baylor's *I'm in Charge of Celebrations*; excerpts from *Seeing the Blue Between: Advice and Inspiration for Young Poets*, by Paul B. Janeczko; excerpts from *Speaking of Journals*, edited by Paula Graham; and poems by William Stafford, Mary Oliver, Billy Collins, and others. Poems can provide intense lessons in the writerly life!

Anticipate the Trajectory of Your Students' Work across the Whole Unit

We recommend that students cycle through the writing process twice during this unit. Few fourth-graders have the skills or inclination to write four or five successive drafts of a single piece, which means that if students work on only one piece for four weeks, they may end up making minor revisions to the ending one day, to the character description another day, and that is not close to enough productivity for a day. We have come to believe that the best way to set students up to write a lot, work productively, and cycle through the writing process with confidence and independence is to shepherd them through more cycles of narrative writing. If you choose this path, your students will write entries in their notebook for the first week, producing at least one entry in school and one at home each day. Most of these entries will be at least a page long (you hope longer), and you'll usher children toward not only generating entries but raising the level of their writing. In the second bend of the unit, students will select one of these entries as a "seed idea." They'll spend one or perhaps two days rehearsing for the draft they'll write outside the notebook, drawing on prior experience to story-tell the entry to a partner a number of times. Then, they will spend one intense day producing a fast draft of the story. This will be followed by several days of revision, during which students will make extensive revisions to their first drafts, sometimes rewriting the draft entirely, other times using strips of paper and other methods to insert additions and cutting or reworking other sections. Students will end this weeklong bend by learning a few strategies for editing their writing.

In bend three, students will cycle through the writing process again, this time transferring all they have learned to a second piece of writing. In the end you'll ask students to pick just one piece to publish. Be sure they spend a day or two revising this selected text in significant ways. (Over the course of the unit, explicitly teach them more large-scale and independent revision strategies.) Encourage them to reread, rethink, reimagine, and reenvision their stories. Teach them to decide what meaning they want to put forward and to deliberately write in ways that realize this vision even though they won't be held accountable for this challenging work until fifth grade.

At the end of the unit, children will publish their narrative pieces (see the suggestions below for how to celebrate). You might decide to display children's best pieces individually or create a class anthology. You might invite other classes or children's family members to your room to celebrate your students' work, or you could simply post the work on bulletin boards in the hallway outside your room for passersby to read.

BEND I: GENERATE NARRATIVE WRITING AND RECALL WHAT YOU KNOW

Launch the year with inspiration.

It is impossible to overemphasize the importance of inspiration. Sift through all your teaching memories until you recall a time when your work felt really good to you. Now ask yourself, "What made that particular time in my teaching life so good?" Chances are it was powerful not because you could arrive late and leave early, working without stress or pressure or expectations. Rather, it was likely a time when you believed your input mattered: a time when you felt called upon to give and give and give some more, and you were willing to do so because you believed your work was adding up to something, because you could tell you were affecting others, because you felt appreciated.

Like you, your students need to know that their ideas matter, that their voices count. They need to feel they are doing work that matters and is important to them. To this end, before telling children about the work of this unit (and of the year), invite them to reflect on their lives as writers. Ask them to think and jot quickly about a time in their lives when writing was particularly good or particularly hard, and have them talk in partnerships or tables (two sets of partners) or as a whole class about what they found and what that means for the year ahead. Of course, if you want children to open up to the community in this way, it helps if you do the same. Share a story about when writing was good or hard for you. To do this, use your narrative writing skills to intensify the event. Children will be more apt to respond with their own stories.

The goal, of course, is to move beyond this to thinking, "How can we make this into the best possible year for us as writers, one in which all of us feel supported?" Be sure children understand that you, too, are a member of this writing community—that you are a passionate writer. Bring your own notebook to class and be prepared to share how writing makes you into a more reflective person.

Guide students to study mentor texts and rely on a repertoire of known strategies to generate entries.

From Day One, you'll want to rally children around the goal of creating powerful writing. You might say, "Writers, it's important to remember you are writing for readers—your writing needs to be as true and as meaningful as it can be, so your words stop readers in their tracks and they go, 'Ahhh.'" You might begin the unit by immersing students in strong narrative writing, asking them to name the qualities they recognize in these stories. Teach them that writers study the craft of writers they admire and ask, "What did this author do that I could also do to make my own writing more powerful?" This sort of thinking about writerly intent is important in the CCSS, and to your children's progress. Children may discuss these craft moves with their writing partners, sharing what they noticed in the texts they read and then selecting the work they will tackle as they write. This analysis of craft supports both children's writing and their reading skills; reflecting on authors' practice and intent leads to reading with deeper comprehension and also triggers awareness of audience (and thus higher-level writing). This means that even at the beginning of this unit, you will nudge your kids to think in ways that hit levels 3 and 4 on Norman L. Webb's Depth of Knowledge scale and to consider how to apply to their own work the skills they analyze as valuable in published writing.

During the first week of this unit, you'll teach children strategies for generating ideas and entries in their notebooks. If most of your children were in writing workshops during third grade, you'll remind them of their repertoire of strategies from those workshops. Either way, tell children that this year, you will not only teach them new strategies for collecting ideas but also teach them how to use familiar strategies *really well*, like professional writers do. Encourage children to share strategies they already know and compile these on a chart titled "Strategies for Generating Narrative Writing." We recommend you *do not* dust off a chart you used during previous years. Children should see their own ideas and words (and yours as well) going onto chart paper and feel that those charts capture the contours of their lived experience in this new classroom.

Your job during this first week, then, is not only to help children generate ideas and write entries but also to lift the level of the work they do with those strategies. For instance, although the children may already know that writers sometimes think of a person that matters, then list several small moments they've experienced with that subject, and choose one of these moments to write as a story, they may not realize that writers take *no more than five minutes* to complete that process. Teach them that the process of brainstorming does not encompass one day's writing workshop. Instead, a writer uses a strategy to generate an idea for writing and writes the entry. Sometimes the writer even has time to return to the original brainstorming list, select a second idea, and write another entry.

If children do use the strategy of listing small moments they spent with a person and then selecting one moment to write in full, encourage them to be sure that their original list of small moments is a list of long phrases, not single words. That is, a child will have a better basis for producing a focused narrative if rather than writing *baseball* under the name *Joe*, the child writes, "The time when Joe taught me how to catch a baseball." Writers select moments that grip them, ones that make them feel something intensely. As the saying goes, "No tears for the writer, no tears for the reader."

Teach strategies that channel children to write about especially significant moments.

Plan to teach strategies that channel children toward writing pieces that are especially significant to them. Likewise, writers can look at their surroundings and let the objects and people around them spark memories. The kitchen table might conjure images of a particularly special Thanksgiving meal or a big fight the child had with his or her sister. The dog bed in the corner might remind a child of the day they brought their new puppy home. Finally, teach your class that stories of significance may be found in the smallest and most seemingly ordinary occasions—a ladybug alighting on your hand before flying away or a friend asking to play video games together.

Although you may teach one particular strategy for generating writing on a given day, when the children write, some of them will use strategies from previous days. Others will not need any strategy; they'll come to the desk or table ready to write. Still others will continue writing an entry started on an earlier day. Take a count one day. How many of the kids are using the strategy you taught that day? It should be *less than half*. If most of your class routinely does only what you teach in that day's minilesson, remind them that writers draw on their full repertoire of strategies. Also check that you are not inadvertently conveying the message, "Wait until I get you started on today's piece of writing." It is crucial that children begin writing without leaning on your approval or on a single day's teaching, that they readily transfer and apply their repertoire of strategies as they work, and that they do so with independence.

Another word of caution: don't overload children with too many strategies. Any one strategy can be applied over and over and over, so children do not need many. Of course, it's okay if in just one day you lay out several possible strategies for generating writing. You could, for example, demonstrate one in the minilesson, another in your mid-workshop teaching point, and still another in your share. However, it is important that over time children rely less and less on strategies for generating writing, coming to regard life itself as one big source of stories! As soon as your children are living like writers, they'll find that true stories spring to mind all on their own—that everything and anything they see and do and think and feel can remind them of stories they have to tell.

Lift the level of students' narrative entries even before they write draft one.

After devoting two days to strategies for generating writing, children will have plenty to draw from, and you will be free to address the next challenge: lifting the level of their writing.

Teach children to examine and diagnose their entries as a doctor would diagnose a patient, thinking, "Have I done everything I have learned to do to make this a strong piece of writing?"

You will probably need to teach or reteach the essentials of narrative writing. Let children know that narratives are just that—stories. In a personal narrative, one character (presumably the writer) experiences one thing, then the next, and then the next. Then remind them that their narratives will be far more effective if they zoom in to a small episode, telling the detailed chronology of that one twenty-minute-or-so episode. A successful entry will not summarize the entire visit to Grandma's farm but will rather focus on the part of the visit when the pigs got loose. "Zooming in" allows a writer to relive an episode with enough detail that the reader, too, can experience it. Don't skip these reminders! They may be basics, but they are fundamental to students' being able to develop real experiences into shapely narratives. Using effective writing techniques, descriptive details, and clear event sequences are all skills emphasized by the Common Core.

After reviewing the basics, you might show students a finished piece of narrative writing that is just a notch or two better than their own and, together, you and your students can study that piece of writing. Teach them to read it closely, much like they would study a complex text in reading, and encourage them to annotate the qualities they see in it. The narrative checklist can help you illuminate the qualities of good writing for children. You may want to use not only the checklist that seems a bit ambitious for most of your children, but also one of the pieces that matches that grade level. You can channel children to ask, "What did that writer do that I can do, too?" Seeing and naming what constitutes strong writing can often clarify children's own goals. As they continue writing in their notebooks, they can set their purpose, aiming to incorporate all that they know about narrative writing from the very start of the writing process. From the first day, then, you'll ask students to reach toward the goal of writing powerful stories—stories that will make readers gasp or laugh aloud or blink back tears.

BEND II: SELECT A FIRST SEED IDEA AND TAKE A PIECE THROUGH THE WRITING PROCESS

Channel students to select a seed idea and rehearse for writing.

Teach children to reread their entries so as to choose one to develop. Each writer can star his or her selected entry. Then you'll teach writers some strategies for rehearsing before drafting. Children could begin by making movies in their minds of what happens in their narratives and then tell the parts of their stories to themselves or to a partner. They'll want to be sure to use storyteller voices as they do this and to tell what happens, bit by bit, weaving action with dialogue, rather than merely providing a commentary on the events. As children become more experienced, they can do more and more rehearsal. Most fourth-graders profit from a reminder that writers often take a few minutes to plan their writing. Tell them, "If you're writing a nonfiction book, you plan by making outlines with main ideas and supportive evidence. But when you are writing narratives, the easiest way to plan is to make timelines or blank books, and then to story-tell as you progress down the timeline or across the pages. Encourage students to story-tell many times, telling the story in a concrete way using one beginning and then another."

Remember that the whole point of this is to get students to plot different ways a story might go. If they rehearse by creating timelines, it is helpful to continually revise those timelines, thinking, "Which dot on the timeline [or which page in the sketch booklet] is not essential to the heart of my story? Which needs to be expanded (by slowing time down) into a series of dots [pages]?" Eventually, children will learn that decisions about what to include and what to bypass, what to stress and what to skip, need to be informed by the message the writer wants to put forward. It may still be too complex to try to convey that the question "How do I start my story?" really can't be answered, save in tandem with the question "What is it I really want my reader to know and feel?"

It is important to raise the level of children's storytelling as they prepare to write. Teach them to plan a story with a beginning, a middle, and an end, and before they tell the story, to think, "What do I want my listener to feel?" You might also teach that storytellers stretch out the good parts, trying to be sure these parts really capture the listener's attention.

Finally, children can rehearse for writing by drafting a lot of different leads. Teach children that writers often start a story with dialogue, with a small action, or by conveying the setting. Again, the real purpose of this instruction is not just to teach students to produce a more dramatic lead; it is also meant to dissuade students from summarizing events and move them toward making movies in their minds. Then, too, since your goal is to lift the level of students' writing, encourage them to think meaningfully about what that bit of dialogue or precise action might be. What will not only draw the reader in right away but also convey something about what's to follow? The child writing about wanting a bike might first try out a lead in which he watches longingly as his friend zips by on a fancy new red bike. Or it might begin with him asking a store owner how much a particular bike costs and then realizing that his allowance savings don't begin to make a dent in that amount.

As children consider different possible leads to their stories, you might suggest that they also consider how their stories will end. Teach them that a story's ending often mirrors a story's beginning (some will have learned this in the second-grade *Lessons from the Masters* unit) and that they can choose to end their story at a moment in the true episode that harkens back to the beginning. That is, just as a piece can begin at any point during an episode, it can also end at any point. Encourage children to rehearse ending their pieces at different places in the course of events, trying to find the point that brings the story to a natural, meaningful conclusion.

Guide children to write, revise, and edit draft one.

Once a writer has drafted and revised timelines that outline the sequence of the events, written a few possible leads for the story, and told the story a handful of times, it's time to draft the story. We strongly suggest children write the whole draft, nonstop, in a single day's writing workshop. Our experience is that stories tend to be vastly more coherent and powerful when they are written quickly, under pressure, in one sitting. Some teachers may lean toward asking a few students to write their drafts in story booklets, and we agree that the booklets help those who need extra scaffolding. However, we're convinced that single sheets are better for helping writers get lost in the rush of a story.

After a one-day fast draft, you'll want to teach children a few strategies for revising. One way to revise is to redraft. One simple way to teach children to write this way is to suggest that they consider their senses (this harkens back to the work some children will have done as second-graders in the *Lessons from the Masters* unit). They can aim to story-tell so that readers can hear what the characters say (or any other sounds they hear), see what they see, smell what they smell, taste what they taste, feel what they feel. It should be possible to imagine movement in the story; who is doing what? A story that incorporates the senses might sound like this: "I walked toward my bedroom and grabbed the doorknob. *It felt cold.* I opened the door and faced the dark room. *I couldn't see anything.*" With just two mentions of what she feels and sees (or, in this case, *doesn't* see), this writer has created a scene that pulls readers into that same experience; readers, too, shiver facing that dark room.

Equally essential to a successful narrative is a combination of inner and outer story. Always, actions should be interwoven with thoughts and feelings, so that the reader can follow not just what is physically happening in the story but also what the writer is experiencing internally. The above story, then, with these elements added, might read like this: "I walked toward my bedroom and grabbed the doorknob. It felt cold. I opened the door and faced the dark room. I couldn't see anything. *I thought, 'This time I will not be afraid.'*"

Many children will tend to stick doggedly to the initial timelines they have created, and you may need to nudge them to revise in larger-scale ways. You may need to tell them that the magic of writing will not happen if they follow their timelines so strictly. Teach them that good writing comes with a strong dose of imagination. Writers make a movie in their minds, and put that whole story onto the page, only to realize that, in fact, it would work better if they tweaked something in their original plan. For example, a writer who is telling the story of going roller skating with her dad may decide that the first dot on her timeline is putting on her skates. She'll picture the drama of doing that, act it out in her mind, and then write: "I arrived early at Skate Key, carrying my roller skates. All the benches were empty so I sat on the first one I saw. I stuck one foot into a roller skate, and pulled the strap tight around my ankles. The skate felt tight. I wondered if my feet had grown. I wiggled my toes. They felt tight." Although she has written with details that allow her reader to picture the scene, experiencing it with her, perhaps this child will realize that the fact that she's outgrowing her skates isn't what's most important to this particular story. Perhaps she'll decide that it's the prospect of spending time with her dad, who lives far away and whom she doesn't know well. She might then try starting her story in the moment when she first sees her dad. Maybe her skates are already on, already tight, and she realizes that she's grown a lot since she was last with him. The more children experiment with their timelines, the more they will get at the truth and the heart of the story they are telling.

While children draft and revise, you'll want them to keep in mind that they won't want to stop and mull over every word they've written. It will be important for them, for example, to spell their best as they write and *move on*. When children know that they have misspelled a word, they are often reluctant to let it go. Teach them to circle or underline a word they want to check later and to move on. If you'd like a bit more attention to spelling as your students draft, you can suggest they write the word three different ways on a sticky note or scrap paper and pick the one that seems closest—and move on.

Then too, you'll want to explicitly teach children a few editing strategies. Some of these can be incorporated into drafting, and some are best used once a draft is done. Remind children to take time as they draft, for example, to correctly spell the high-frequency words they almost know. You'll no doubt have a word wall of words your students "use and confuse"; encourage children to rely on the word wall.

Once a draft is finished, it's reasonable for the writer to reread and check more closely for errors. At this point, you'll want to help children transfer what they learn during word study to their writing. That is, you might turn learned spelling patterns and rules into editing minilessons or items on a checklist that children use. You might also decide to do some work around comma usage, helping students understand the ways commas can be used to create longer, more complex sentences by stringing together shorter thoughts.

Before ending this bend, find a small way to celebrate the work writers have done. Despite the fact that they won't yet publish this piece of writing, there is much to celebrate. You might create an occasion for students to read their writing aloud in small groups. Regardless of how you choose to celebrate, be sure to acknowledge the work students have done and rally them for another round of writing!

BEND III: TRANSFERENCE AND APPLICATION: GO THROUGH THE WRITING PROCESS AGAIN WITH GREATER INDEPENDENCE

Support independence as writers begin anew.

In Bend III, you will cycle children through the writing process again, this time with greater independence. From Day One you'll want to encourage students to transfer and apply all they have learned over the past few weeks. You may decide to give children the opportunity to collect entries again for a few days, but likely you'll begin this bend by having them choose a new seed idea and move immediately to rehearsal.

You might gather your class and remind them that they are the bosses of their writing lives and they need to decide how best to develop this next piece of writing. Before children begin writing each day, you might give them time to brainstorm, help you create tools to monitor their progress, or draw self-assignment boxes in their notebooks. Above all, you want to convey that they will be drawing on all they have already learned. As you watch your writers begin the process anew, teach them to solve their own problems rather than wait for you. Remind them of pertinent charts or tools or mentor texts that can support them, and help children imagine the best ways to use these tools.

Channel students to draft, revise, and edit.

Once children have chosen a second seed idea, you'll immediately want to launch them into rehearsal and drafting. As in Bend II, children will want to take time to rehearse, and as part of that, they'll imagine different ways their stories might go. This time around you might emphasize the important of meaning. Writers ask, "What is this story really about?" Then, they tell their story a few different ways, attempting to bring forth that meaning.

When drafting, students should feel as if they are reliving the event; their goal will be to let their pens fly, writing on and on and on, capturing the truth of the experience. Remind children that they will have just one day to write their entire drafts and that they are to keep their hands moving as they relive the events. As you move among the children, look for students who are summarizing instead of story-telling. If you can, intervene now and help them get started with an entirely new draft. This work should feel seamless to kids; with all the rehearsal work they've done, their pens should be racing down the page, trying to keep up with their fleshed-out stories.

Another very important reason to ask children to start and finish a single draft all in one day is that doing so will likely mean they will not be as wedded to this draft as they would be if they'd eked it out across a week of work. Even if they have not completed this draft, suggest that they pause after a day of drafting to imagine a very different way their draft could be written. Almost always, despite their best efforts to zoom in, young writers will stride over too much terrain, writing with big steps. They'll tend to talk about rather than relive an event and bypass a huge amount of detail that is essential to an engaging narrative.

Emphasize that revision is not about making teeny, tiny changes at the sentence or word level. At this stage in their writing careers, after they've made it through a whole first draft, they can step back and ask, "What else can I do to bring out the meaning of this story to my reader?" You'll want to set children up to plan for and then write what will be an almost entirely new draft. Probably the new draft will be more focused, more detailed. There may be other ways to improve the draft, too, and the narrative checklist can help students consider those improvements. Then set children up to write a second draft, again writing fast and furious. This draft, too, will deserve revision.

For example, the Common Core State Standards for narrative writing expect fourth-graders to orient the reader. That is, students at this age need to establish a situation and introduce the narrator or characters in a story. It is easiest to write a line or two that does this after the draft is already written. We suggest, therefore, that you teach children to reread their writing and think, "Does my reader know when and where this is happening?" In most instances, the situation will be clear to the reader. In order to write a good lead, it can also help if writers think about what they really want readers to know about this one episode. For example, a child who is writing a story about riding a roller coaster can think, "What's important to know about this particular ride on the roller coaster?" If she says that it was her first time riding it and that she was *terrified*, she might start her story with, "It was the summer I was going to face the roller coaster. All my friends rode it without being scared, so this time, I am going to do that, too." That is, she can put forward not only the physical setting, but also she can let the reader know what's so important about *this* one time for *this* writer.

The key to tackling this work successfully is that kids write just a line or two about why this event matters and they do not throw out all they have learned about using dialogue or small actions to create good leads. Usually after the one- or two-line orientation, writers plunge into storytelling, and do so by starting with dialogue or a small action.

You may notice that some children's drafts are swamped with dialogue. Often readers can't even discern who is speaking or what is happening. In these instances, it is likely that writers haven't yet mastered how to translate what they see in the movies in their minds to their own writing. Over-reliance on dialogue represents a step forward but will need to be addressed. Teach these children that sometimes after writing a draft, a writer realizes that her writing provides only a sound track, and so she revises it to show other aspects of the story—actions, thoughts, description—that she left out. Remind these kids that good writing comes from a mix of thought, action, and dialogue. You might explain it this way: "Think about what you do over the course of the day. Do you talk endlessly? No way! You also *do* things and *think* things and *feel* things. It's like that for the 'you' you're putting onto the page, too." If writers have a sense of the various strands that are woven together in a narrative, their writing will become stronger.

Remind children to draw on all they already know about revision. The most important revision will involve rereading and asking, "Where is the heart of my story?" Writers then stretch out that part of the story, writing it with more detail. When students do this, it helps if they tell both the external *and* the internal story, so that readers can experience not only what they recall about the action of an episode but also what they thought and felt at that moment.

Emphasize that writers need to reflect on what is working in their writing and then make plans based on their reflections. Help writers use one another as critical friends. You might use your teaching shares as opportunities for your children to discuss with each other ways to make their writing better. Writers might approach their partners with ideas for what to work on, and then their partners might give suggestions on how to do so. As writing workshop draws to a close, teach children that writers set their plans for the next day's writing, so that increasingly, students set their own agendas rather than expect you to do so in minilessons.

The real goal is to improve the quality of the writing—*and* the writers. Your deeper lesson throughout the unit will be this: writers never stop learning how to write better. It is not enough to learn that an author includes dialogue (or internal thinking or setting) and to then add that one thing, checking it off an imaginary to-do list. Rather, children should learn that to be a successful writer means to be engaged in the long-term continual study of good writing and good writing habits.

Wrap up the unit.

After revising and editing their second stories, students will choose one of their drafts to take all the way to publication. They will do large-scale revision on this piece, creating entirely new drafts as you, using mentor texts, teach them to reimagine and relive the story and to story-tell to evoke emotion and bring out meaning. As you near the end of the unit, encourage students to use their best analytical skills to evaluate which of the newly acquired revision strategies will work best in this piece. Teach what you notice students forgetting, and further raise the level of their work. Remind your writers to consider their personal goals and push themselves to make this piece of writing better than before. You can draw on later narrative units in this series and on the narrative writing learning progression to support this work.

Celebrate!

Publishing might happen in a variety of ways, such as a publishing celebration in which the students' narratives are placed on their desktops or tabletops alongside a blank sheet of loose-leaf paper. Students then move around, reading their peers' work and offering positive comments. Narratives might also be posted on bulletin boards or on hallway walls. Classroom anthologies might be assembled and earn a place in the classroom library. These are just suggestions. You are free to imagine and create ways to celebrate and go public with student work. You may want to devote another day to an on-demand writing assignment. If you do, give your children the very same directions you gave at the start of the year, only this time let them know you want to see what they have learned from the month of studying narrative writing. Then, once again, be sure to insist they work with independence.

Information Writing
Writing about Topics of Personal Expertise

RATIONALE/INTRODUCTION

The Common Core State Standards highlight the importance of information (or explanatory) writing, describing this as writing that is designed to "examine a topic and convey information and ideas clearly." In information writing, the driving structure is apt to be categories and subcategories: topics and subtopics that are signaled with headings and subheadings and with accompanying information portals, including glossaries; text boxes or sidebars; and diagrams, charts, graphs, and other visuals. If you have cycled through the second- and third-grade units on information writing, your students will now be well positioned to write information texts about topics that are research-based. The fourth-grade volume *Bringing History to Life* assumes your students have the body of knowledge in information writing to do the job of writing texts on the American Revolution—a job that requires the acquisition, processing, and restructuring of outside information.

If your students, in an on-demand assessment, demonstrate that they cannot introduce a topic clearly, separate it into subtopics, and organize their writing so that appropriate information is grouped together inside their subtopics, then you may want to teach this unit before embarking on *Bringing History to Life*. In this unit, you'll give children the opportunity to strengthen their information writing skills by writing about areas of personal expertise—their hobbies. In this way, you free yourself (and your teaching) to focus predominantly on the structuring of information texts, not research.

You'll channel students to work toward creating lively, voice-filled, engaging information books about topics in which they are deeply invested.

Whatever the form of nonfiction writing, a key component of this genre is structure, and a good portion of your teaching will focus on this important element of writing. According to CCSS W.4.2a, fourth-grade information writers should be able to group related information in paragraphs and sections and include formatting (e.g., headings) when needed. Additionally, CCSS W.4.2c urges fourth-graders to work toward creating cohesive structures in their information writing by using linking words and phrases as a way to connect information within sections. They should also develop topics and subtopics with facts, definitions, and other information related to the topic. CCSS W.4.2a and W.4.2e also remind us that fourth-grade writers should introduce their topics clearly and should, at the end of their pieces, provide a concluding statement or section related to the information presented.

Because information texts are usually composites of smaller texts/chapters that are often written in different text structures and genres, any unit on information writing is bound to stand on the shoulders of units in narrative, opinion, and procedural writing, as well as on units in nonfiction reading. This unit aims to help students harness all they know about all of these kinds of writing, using all this knowledge in the service of creating texts that teach readers. You will want to turn to the Information Writing Checklists for third and fourth grade as a way to assess where your students are and as a resource for teaching.

A SUMMARY OF THE BENDS IN THE ROAD FOR THIS UNIT

In Bend I (Structure Information Writing), students will decide quickly on a topic of personal expertise and begin imagining how a book about that subject might go. They will study mentor texts, try out a variety of tables of contents, and then plan the content of each chapter. They will learn to rehearse for their writing by "teaching" their topic orally, focusing on being organized and using an expert tone. As students begin drafting the chapters of their books, you'll show them how to try on several different organizational structures. By the end of Bend I, students will have drafted a good portion of their information books.

In Bend II (Make Big, Strong Revisions), students will learn to revise their information books on many levels. They will begin by studying the art of big, structural revision—learning to be deliberate about how they divided and subdivided their topics, and providing a strong foundation for their content. Students will also learn to imagine gaps in the content they have provided (and write new chapters to address those gaps), elaborate further, and play with the craft and tone of their writing. The students will have mentor texts on hand, and you'll teach them to study these texts through a writer's eye, asking, "What has this author done that I might try also?"

In Bend III (Write a Feature Article), students will use all they have learned about structure, organization, elaboration, and revision of information texts to write in a new genre—feature articles. They'll learn that while before they structured information using chapters and subsections, they will now focus their attention on writing a smaller text, with subsections and paragraphs. With this new focus comes new challenges. As in the prior two bends, students will be encouraged to write about topics on which they have some knowledge or expertise.

GETTING READY

Assess Information Writing

Before embarking on this unit you will probably decide to begin with an on-demand information writing assessment. If you do, we recommend using the same prompt and same conditions as other teachers have used, which can be found in *Writing Pathways: Performance Assessments and Learning Progressions, K–5*. This means that on the day before the assessment, you might say to your students, "Think of a topic that you've studied or know about. Tomorrow, you will have forty-five minutes to write an informational (or all-about) text that teaches others interesting and important information and ideas about that topic. If you want to find and use information from a book or another outside source, you may bring that with you tomorrow. Please keep in mind that you'll have forty-five minutes to complete this. You will only have this one period, so you'll need to plan, draft, revise, and edit in one sitting. Write in a way that shows me all you know about information writing."

You might also give your writers a few extra reminders. We suggest reminding them that they should:

- Write a beginning that gets readers interested in the subject and sets them up to learn more about it.

- Include facts and details (examples, anecdotes, statistics, expert words) to teach readers important information and ideas about the subject.

- Organize their writing to best teach readers about their subjects and use transition words (*for example, in contrast, another*) to help readers understand how the different bits of information go together.

- Write an ending, ideally one that reminds readers why this subject is important.

This on-demand writing will help you know where your students fall in a trajectory of writing development and set your sights on very clear next steps. Your hope is that at the end of this year, your students' work mostly aligns to the fourth-grade Information Writing Checklist. Now, early in the year, you'll want to see if their work matches the third-grade checklist. If it doesn't yet meet many of these expectations, teach first toward the third-grade checklist. Plan to make rapid progress!

This on-demand writing should also help students realize that information writing is well within their grasp, not something that requires days and weeks of preparation. Most teachers who have done the on-demand assessment have been pleasantly surprised by how much their students bring into this unit of study and by the volume of writing they are able to produce in just one day's writing workshop. The work that students produce in the on-demand situation becomes the baseline, and you can increase expectations as the unit progresses.

Choose Touchstone Texts that Resemble the Kinds You Hope the Children Will Produce

You will probably want to search through your nonfiction texts to find two or three that can become exemplars for your work with informational writing. As you make this choice, you need not think about the *topics* of the texts but instead about the *organizational structures* and the nature of the prose. You'll want to choose texts that resemble those you hope your children will write. For example, if you choose a book about mushrooms that opens with a table of contents that includes chapters that tell about different kinds of mushrooms, as well as one that recounts a day collecting mushrooms, and perhaps include a final chapter that functions as a plea to mushroom lovers of the world, this text could be a mentor text for children who are writing about soccer, flat-coated retrievers, or ballet.

If you have decided to highlight a few features in your unit, then you'll want to make sure the touchstone texts you select illustrate those features. For example, given that you'll probably emphasize the importance of categorizing information, you'll probably want to find model texts that have clear subcategories, with the information pertaining to one subtopic falling under one heading and the information pertaining to another subtopic falling under a second heading. You may decide to look for writers who integrate facts with opinions and ideas. You may also search for exemplar texts in which an author writes with a vigorous voice. This means you'll look for books that engage the reader and sound as though the author is speaking straight to the reader.

As you look for these mentor texts, we strongly suggest you go onto the Teachers College Reading and Writing Project (TCRWP) website to find texts that other children have written. These will, of course, be closer to those your own young writers are apt to write than the texts written by professional authors—and your children may decide to produce their own texts that can replace those on the website!

BEND I: STRUCTURE INFORMATION WRITING

Research consistently finds information writing to be more challenging for children than narrative. Many kids can tell stories, or spin a yarn, before ever entering school, so the structural elements of narrative feel instinctively familiar—character, setting, conflict and its resolution. Information writing, on the other hand, often requires knowledge of unfamiliar content (the tundra, an extinct species, a far-off planet) that is framed in an equally unfamiliar structure. No wonder then, that a *story* about a saber-tooth tiger that, once upon a time, lived in the tundra feels far easier than a *feature article* detailing this animal's causes of extinction. Teaching children to become confident, adept writers of information texts requires teaching them to recognize and re-create the structures in which information writing is framed. For this reason, in Bend I you will focus on teaching organization and structure.

Help students get started: choose a topic and plan for writing.

Research also backs the logic that something new or challenging is best understood when it is couched in something known and familiar. To keep writers' full focus on the organization and structure of the information genre, therefore, you'll want to ensure that they choose topics that feel accessible, easy, and familiar. To this end, you'll want to issue an invitation to children to write about something they are experts on—a topic on which they are an authority. For example, you could say, "If you have three brothers, you could think, 'I could teach a course (or write a book) called *Brothers*.'" One approach is to invite children to brainstorm a favorite hobby—playing soccer, collecting rocks, playing video games, tending a fish tank—and suggest that they consider teaching this topic to others. Another approach is to remind them of a place they visit often—a city, a neighborhood, or the interesting insides of a parent's workplace (a hospital, park, or restaurant). "It has to be a topic you know a lot about," you'll remind them, "because you'll be teaching it to others."

Writers need an end in mind—a vision of the product they'll be creating. You'll tell children that they'll be authoring their own information books, just like the ones they see on the library shelves. You'll want to showcase a few mentor texts, particularly ones with a clear structure that your writers can easily identify. You will probably want to choose one that contains a table of contents that introduces and divides the chapters, each of which takes up a different aspect of the topic. After all, writers don't just throw everything they know about a topic on top of the page in a giant hodgepodge; they divide their knowledge up into different categories, writing with some completeness about one subtopic before approaching another. Of course, the table of contents is not as crucial as the presence of a clear organization structure; nevertheless, it will make this concept especially accessible to your students, so we recommend you choose texts with clear tables of contents.

It is helpful to set writers up for a quick practical rehearsal of their writing and to provide an immediate, very real audience. Once their topics have been chosen, therefore, you'll ask children to begin teaching their topics orally to friends seated beside them. Allow them a few minutes to prepare for this teaching by collecting some thoughts in their notebooks—a process you might want to model. "Since my topic is 'running a classroom,'" you might say as you jot the phrase on the board, "and I have to teach new teachers about it, I'll have to think of some smaller things that go with this big topic." You might then count off subtopics that fall under this umbrella. "This is a big job," you'll tell kids. "It has many parts—like knowing all the children's names and personalities. And learning what to teach them. And finding books to put in the class library." You might jot these subtopics as a list or make spokes that stem like spider legs from the main topic or use any graphic form that illustrates that they are smaller parts of a bigger topic.

After giving children a few minutes to brainstorm and jot subtopics, you'll waste no time in moving them toward teaching a friend. Because the critical focus is on structure, you might insist that while they teach their topics, they use the fingers of one hand as a graphic organizer. Hold up your own hand and demonstrate: "Count off points on your fingers as you teach. One point about my topic is . . . Another point about my topic is . . . A third point about this topic is . . ." The simple act of moving on from one finger to the next can propel children into listing several points instead of lingering endlessly on one point. You want writers to develop a broad structure for their writing before they begin elaborating on the details; you'll demand breadth before depth. "Imagine you're counting off the different points in the table of contents of your book—the different big things about this topic that you can imagine teaching." Once your writers have several subtopics at their fingertips, you can push them to go deeper by telling their friends a few sentences about each of these subtopics. "Go back over each subtopic that you just counted out, starting from the first," you'll direct, "only this time, linger at each finger and say a few sentences about this subtopic."

As they "teach" their topics, urge children to talk like the experts they are. "If I have to teach someone about running a classroom," you might say, "I'll certainly be using some technical teaching language, words like *assessment* or *comprehension* or *rubric*. You'll want to use the technical language of *your* topic while teaching."

This oral rehearsal for writing—topic selection and subsequent collecting of thoughts—shouldn't take very long, especially since you have scaffolded this work with guided instruction and peer support. Don't waste a day before pushing youngsters into the actual work of writing. You'll want children to get their thoughts and structure down on paper before they have a chance to lose focus.

Once children have a basic structure of headings and subheadings down, they might consider developing each subheading into its own chapter or they might narrow their writing focus by picking a subheading as their big topic to write about. Again, the best thing you can do is use your own writing to model whatever you want children to do, so bring out your own topic (running a classroom) and demonstrate that one of your subtopics can in fact be a big enough topic in its own right. In this way you'll show writers that they may narrow their topic. From your original table of contents:

Running a Classroom

- Organizing the teaching and learning space in a room
- Deciding what to teach
- Planning lessons

you might narrow down to a subtopic, make this your new topic, and consequently devise a new table of contents.

Organizing the Teaching and Learning Space

- Centers
- Read-aloud corner and rug
- Cubbies
- Sink and art supplies

You'll be wise to coach your stronger writers toward more focused topics. The subject *baseball pitcher* will make for better writing than *baseball*, but the more focused subject will also be more challenging. You might decide to teach children that writers "try on" ideas by brainstorming subtopics they could include in a particular nonfiction text.

Channel students to revise plans, then begin to draft.

You might also decide to teach several variations of subheadings. Mentor texts can be an invaluable resource to mine for specific subheadings, and you can draw attention to the ways these branch out from the main topic. Instead of asking partners to look at a mentor text in its entirety, have them isolate and look only at the subheadings in a book and study those. For example, a book about rainforests might have the subheading "Types of Rainforests" or "Kinds of Animals that Live in Rainforests" or even "Ways to Save the Rainforest." Writers may notice that subheadings often show the types or kinds of something and that they also depict the ways things happen.

Think of any composite structure: a model airplane, a dollhouse, or a train track. You'll realize that structure relies not only on bits and parts but also on the logic and planning of how these parts fit together. Early on, while writers are still in the rehearsal stage, therefore, be aware that the smaller parts, or points, of their topic must connect with one another or be arranged in a way that grants sense to the larger structure. One way to help children begin to wrestle with the logic that undergirds their texts is to demand the use of transitions—connecting words that link. Words and phrases such as *also* and *in addition* show that the text is structured in an additive way. *On the other hand* or *but* show that the things laid beside each other are different. Transition words nudge writers into the awareness that one point can extend, exemplify, or contradict another. It is a good idea to encourage the deliberate use of transitions during conferring and small-group work.

Meanwhile, you'll want to push writers into *actually writing*. Don't be surprised if you find a youngster who wants to endlessly hash and rehash a structure/table of contents without getting any content down. You'll need to spur your writers into taking the plunge and starting on the content that they plan to write. "You will have plenty of time to make it perfect," you'll reassure them. "These headings and subheadings will get you started, and you'll only know how well they work once you begin writing out the chapters of your books, long and strong. Later, you can revise, but first you must write, write, write!"

Even as you push for volume, however, you'll want to maintain your focus on organization and structure. To show students ways they can try out different chapters in their writer's notebooks, you'll want to draw on what they might already know from writing in the content areas. If you have taught webbing, timelines, T-charts, or flowcharts, use those to talk about the structure of a chapter or a book. Remind writers how these text structures work; for example, a flowchart might document everything a baseball pitcher does in a typical game, whereas a T-chart could be used to compare and contrast what the pitcher and the batter do in an at-bat. Encourage writers to include text features, such as annotated sketches, to develop their chapters; for example, the writer might draw the pitcher and pitcher's mound as a way to show information.

You may want to lay out multiple paper options for students to choose from as they draft. In addition, you'll want to teach students that the paper they choose should be based on the structure they think matches this particular chapter's information. For example, in a book about gymnastics, a chapter about the different events could be written in boxes and bullets underneath the topic sentence "There are many different events in the sport of gymnastics." If the writer chooses this structure, he will probably need a page full of lines for writing. However, a writer might instead choose to put this information into an annotated diagram of a gymnasium, labeling and describing the events. In this case, he is looking for a sheet of paper with a huge picture box. Or the writer could choose two events to compare and contrast, such as the men's bar and the women's bar. In this case, he might imagine paper that has two side-by-side picture boxes with lines underneath.

A study of mentor texts will reveal that there can be multigenre sections or chapters in informational books. For example, students might notice that within a book about pet fish, there is a chapter or section on cleaning a fish tank and that this section is written in a procedural, or how-to, structure. Or they may notice that even in a nonfiction book, there are often times when information is delivered through a story or vignette. Similarly, there are often times when an author chooses to put forth a specific idea or opinion using a more persuasive type of writing, with a claim followed by supports. You can help your writers see that within a book about gymnastics, they could write a single chapter entitled "Too Dangerous for Young Girls" or "Gymnastics Helps Girls Stay Healthy" with supports for the claim. Many teachers channel young writers to make their last chapter a plea to make a real-world difference relative to the topic. Children might conclude with "People Should Take Better Care of Their Pets" or "Soccer Teaches You Sportsmanship" or "Beagles Are the Best Dogs in the World." Either way, the writer of such a chapter will be practicing writing persuasive essays.

Support volume and teach elaboration.

You'll aim for students to have completed three or four chapters of their informational booklets by the end of the first bend. To this end, encourage them to write a "chapter" a day, even if this chapter is less than a page in length. It isn't perfection that you're aiming for. These "books" will help writers develop a mental model for the structure of an informational text. You'll move them along, urging them to fill out the content under heading upon heading, within chapter upon chapter, so that they are able to get a feel for writing with breadth about a topic.

You'll probably find that the first chapters your children write are fairly bare-bones, so early on you'll teach students to elaborate. One place to start is by teaching writers that it can help to embed anecdotes into their texts, taking what they know about Small Moment writing to craft little stories that are illustrative of whatever they are teaching. Then, too, it can help to teach writers the discipline of writing in "twin sentences." Often it is good discipline to write a second sentence elaborating on whatever the first sentence said. Say I wrote, "There are many kinds of dogs." I planned to proceed to talk about one kind of dog that I especially love. Before doing so, though, I can say to myself, "I need one more sentence to go with that first one." This time, I write, "There are many kinds of dogs. They are divided into major categories such as hunting dogs, retrieving dogs and the like, and then within each broad category, there are scores of specific breeds."

There are other ways of elaborating. Instead of simply writing a twin sentence (or a partner sentence, if your kids call it that), writers can become accustomed to moving up and down a level of abstraction (although you may not call it that). What we mean is this: if a writer has written a fact, such as "Dogs eat dog biscuits," then the writer can try to write an example: "Dog biscuits are often shaped like little bones." Writers can also elaborate by relating whatever they've just said to something that the reader may know. For example, "Dogs eat dog biscuits. Dog biscuits are like cookies and cakes for your dog."

BEND II: MAKE BIG, STRONG REVISIONS

Writers revise at many levels. Writers revise a word until they get the precise meaning they want to convey. But they also make big revisions—slashing and replacing a paragraph, a page, sometimes an entire chapter—to create a new focus altogether. Similarly, writers revise mid-sentence and mid-thought, before the proverbial ink has had a chance to dry on the page, but they *also* revise published works years after they were first written. Before beginning a bend on revision, you need to be clear about the kind of revision you expect youngsters to do.

You'll want to clarify early on that this is a bend for big-structure revisions. You might use the analogy of an architect who stands back from the skeletal structure of a building to yell, "Halt! That beam is crooked!" or "We need another retaining wall before we build a second story." Structural revision is crucial to the overall piece of writing. Writers revise structure to check whether their writing is balanced, whether it will even stand. Since structure (and organization) was the focus of your teaching in the first bend, this second bend will neatly spiral back over that teaching. You'll want writers to become much more deliberate about how they divide and subdivide their topics. So far, writers have created a small book on a topic of their choice, creating several chapters. You might begin this bend by asking writers to look critically at chapter titles and (if they haven't already done this) to create a table of contents for what they have so far. You might begin your teaching with sequence and order. Urge youngsters to ask themselves, "Does this part of my book go clearly with this other part?" or "Are the parts arranged in the best possible order? Does this chapter belong before this other one?"

To start, you might need to teach them to make sure that their chapters are equal; that is, one chapter can't be a big heading while another represents a tiny subheading. As always, live demonstration using your own piece will go a long way. "Here is the table of contents from my piece on running a classroom," you might say, putting it up on an overhead display.

Running a Classroom

As you read the chapter titles one by one, model confusion over the fourth. Ask aloud, "Is this topic worthy of being a chapter by itself or might it only be a small part of another chapter?" You'll want writers to see that the current Chapter 4 is not a big enough topic to stand alone in its own right next to Chapters 1, 2, and 3. You'll hope that your writers can tell you that it actually belongs as part of Chapter 2. These are big structural revisions. In teaching them, your aim is to push writers into appraising the big picture, the entire landscape of their book. Creating logical structure in a piece of writing requires developing exactly this kind of awareness of text meta-structure.

While they're revising the big structure of their books, you'll want them to question what they *haven't* yet written. "Imagine reading a book about extinct animals and not seeing any mention of dinosaurs." Remind youngsters that a book's title and chapter titles set readers up to *expect* certain content. Have they included all the content that their title suggests? Might they need to add a section? Or might they need to amend and narrow the title instead? "If it was a book entitled *Extinct Mammals*, well then I certainly wouldn't expect to see any dinosaurs in there," you might explain. "Writers make sure that their chapter titles match what is inside. They can change the title—or they can change what is inside!" To extend this teaching, you might also need to explain that writers often reread chapter content and cordon off a portion that may need to go under a separate chapter heading. In doing this, they may come up with an entirely new chapter. You might say, "Revising helps us come up with new chapters, new writing! You know when writers stop in the middle of a piece of writing and think they have writer's block? All they need to do is revise. Pretty soon they'll find that sitting in the middle of what they already have are plenty of other things to write and develop!"

Partnerships can play an invaluable role in this work. In this bend, set children up with a new partner—someone who hasn't helped them with drafting and is new to their book and content—so they can role-play the "outsider" reader. As partners read each other's books, ask them to provide feedback on what the title of a chapter sets them up to expect—perhaps jotting this quickly on a sticky note as they read. Then, instruct partners to read on and provide feedback on whether this expectation was met or not—whether it left them with unanswered questions. This sort of mid-process feedback is a powerful thing. Published writers often credit a spouse or an editor for being their mid-process reviewer, often claiming that "without them, this book might never have been written." A valuable part of establishing a writing community in your classroom is to teach youngsters to be one another's mid-process reviewers and editors. You might need to teach children ways to couch these observations in supportive, constructive language so they don't demoralize their partners, however. Monitor the tone and climate of this work; explain that partners are each other's collaborators or part of each other's writing team, not each other's *critics*.

Providing specific review prompts can channel partners into giving each other feedback that is specific *and* constructive. You might put up a chart to remind writers to provide feedback using the following prompts.

- "This leaves me with the question . . ."
- "Can you give me an example of this?"
- "Can this be shown through a diagram or illustration?"
- "Can there be a part in between to connect [something that came before] with this section?"
- "I was expecting that this part would be about . . . because of [the title of this section/the paragraph before this]. Instead, this part is about . . ."

Specific feedback like this will help youngsters be more mindful of their invisible audience (the reader) and focus their revision efforts.

While the larger emphasis in this bend is on revision, don't neglect volume. The writing children do should match the amount they were generating in the previous bend, if not outdo that amount. Dispel the myth that revising involves tiny flourishes—adjusting the droop of one stem in the vase or the angle of a teaspoon. The kind of deep structural revision that you've been teaching involves rolling up one's sleeves. It will generate its own volume of writing. Expect children to write or rewrite entire chapters, create new subcategories, and add explanatory paragraphs and text features. Monitor the volume of writing they do—understanding that while this volume may not translate into a lengthy final piece (since it may involve crossing out and rewriting), the focus and structure of their revised writing ought to reflect a deliberated, logical sequence of information and ideas.

As they revise in ways that are deliberate and purposeful, you might encourage writers to log their process. Suggest that each day's share involve discussing and jotting the specific revision moves that children made, and ask them to elaborate why they felt the need for a specific revision and whether the revised writing fulfills their intent and purpose. Once you have this sort of self-reflection and self-monitoring going on in the room, you'll have rich potential for powerful conferring and peer discussions.

In time, you may teach writers to be sure they have incorporated the technical language of their topics, to be sure they include diagrams and drawings to help readers understand, to be sure they are writing with precision and detail that will keep their readers' attention, to be sure they've incorporated whatever they admire from published work into their writing, and so forth. Teach writers to look for the gaps in their pieces, searching for places they could say more, spruce up, or even remove.

Children will look to mentor texts throughout the process, but you'll especially use them to show writers how to incorporate the features of this genre into their books. Children will love noticing how the author of a mentor text used illustrations and diagrams as teaching tools. You may also teach children to add other features such as glossaries, indexes, and back-cover blurbs to their finished pieces. During reading workshop, students will have noticed how headings help readers know what's to come and how the font size of these headings and subheadings cues readers to the importance of the information that follows.

You'll want to end this bend with a celebration of the books that your writers have produced. As they publish these books for an audience of peers or parents, you'll specifically congratulate them for having mastered the structure of informational writing. "You can make the parts of a book go together. You're masters of structure now!" you'll say. "And you've proved that you can revise this structure, make it more balanced and complete." It is no small achievement, either, for children to create sense out of chaos, to take all they know about a topic and massage it into a sequence that is logical and elaborated. It is time, now, to turn them toward writing a new, very different kind of informational text.

BEND III: PUTTING IT ALL TOGETHER—WRITING A NEW INFORMATION BOOK

In the first two bends, you channeled children to choose a topic they knew well and focused your teaching on structure, organization, elaboration, and revision. Now that they have created and published one solid round of information books, you will want them to repeat the process a second time, this time holding themselves to higher expectations. Students will draw on their new understanding of both structure and revision in order to write new books that reflect all that they've learned about this kind of writing in the first two bends. That is, they'll "put it all together" in this next round of information books.

Specifically, students will create books that are deliberately researched and thoughtfully organized. They will write chapters divided into approximately like sizes, with each chunk of content organized into one or more of the various structures that best showcases the content and that include text features that best convey the information. They'll make sure that not only their chapters, but also the sentences within each one, are organized clearly in an order that makes sense and that teaches most effectively, and that they've grouped information that goes together, leaving out information that doesn't belong. They'll anticipate what the reader needs to know for each section so that they are sure to include any explanatory information, diagrams, and illustrations. Meanwhile, they'll aim to write with precision and details so as to hold their readers' attention, and to write with elaboration and volume.

In this final bend, then, you'll suggest that students now have the experience and know-how to write even more developed information books on a new topic. Again, you'll encourage them to choose topics about which they have some knowledge and that mean something to them. This might be a place they frequent (e.g., a restaurant, a pool, or a city), a sport they watch and play, a personality they know (a famous public figure or a family member), an animal they're experts on (an extinct animal they've read about or a pet), a hobby or activity they love.

You'll also need to select a new topic for your own information book, which you'll use to demonstrate during minilessons. You might briefly model this process by listing a few possible topics and considering aloud which of these you'd want to pick to write about. You might select a topic that plays into your students' experiences (e.g., parks for children or video games) not only so that you hold their interest when talking about it, but also so that they can take on a more active role during some minilessons, helping you think about and craft your book. Whatever you decide, make sure the topic is one whose content can be structured in a variety of ways, according to the different structures you've taught your class—webbing, timelines, T-charts, flowcharts—so that students continue to consider how structure can be used to bring out different aspects of a topic. This, too, will help them hone their skills of presenting information in specific ways to suit the style and tone of a particular information writing piece.

Teach toward independence.

One big goal of this bend is for students to work with increased independence, so you'll want to encourage and support this. You might suggest that partners rely on some of the tools you introduced earlier, such as the chart of feedback prompts designed to help writers be sure they have been as thorough and clear and informative as possible. Students can also revisit the mentor texts they especially admired earlier in the unit or consult new ones that will best help them construct their new books. While you will, of course, still be on hand to answer questions and help students think through possibilities, you'll encourage them to rely on resources they have in the room and on their own growing skill and confidence as informational writers.

As part of this final bend, you'll want children to find new challenges while honing skills they learned in the first part of the unit. To that end, encourage them to try things they may not have tried during the first two bends. This might mean exploring a different type of topic. For example, a child who wrote an information book about a person might now write an information book about an activity. This new kind of topic choice will likely lead her to incorporate a new type of writing into her piece: how to skateboard, how to play the flute, or how to bake the best chocolate chip cookies. Whereas there may have been no possible cons to writing about his mother, a child might introduce a bit of pro–con exploration in a topic such as contact sports or fast food or having exotic animals as pets.

Children might also aim to incorporate text features they didn't try out in their first information book—or to do so more extensively and with greater detail. Again, they can look to mentor texts, or to one another's first round of published books, for ideas of different ways that information books go that they can now try. They might also talk in partnerships about how to raise the level of expertise of their writing by incorporating text features in more sophisticated ways.

Hone students' skills by delving deeper into structure and text features.

As you think about how to teach this final bend, consider ways you might extend children's understanding and use of structure and text features. To do so, you may need to stretch your own imagination a little! Let's say you chose the topic video games for your demonstration book that will weave throughout this bend. Ask yourself, "How might I explore this topic, not only in obvious ways, but in more unusual ways?" Perhaps you'll come up with ways to model how to incorporate all the structures you've taught the class so far. This might include pros and cons of video games (T-chart), different systems/kinds of video games (webbing), if you and your friend want to play a particular video game (flow chart), how to get ready to play a video game (timeline), and so on. To extend children's thinking, you might teach them that information writers sometimes use structure to come up with subtopics rather than the other way around. You might say, "A T-chart is like a comparison . . . hmmm, I wonder what sort of comparison I could make with my topic, video games . . ." Let that thought linger for a minute, and then say, "Oh! Well, I know that some people think video games are bad for kids, so maybe I could compare what's good about video games with what's not so good about them." Then tap your head, as if thinking, and say, "Oh! I could also compare video games to something else, like board games, or I could compare two different *kinds* of video games (like adventure games and target games), or two different *games*, themselves, like Angry Birds and Early Bird."

One natural exploration children may follow during this final bend is writing with an angle. While you won't want this bend to step on the toes of the essay writing unit of study, you may find that students are inclined to write in ways that bring out their opinion—and you won't want to dampen their enthusiasm or dissuade them from writing to bring out an angle. After all, that is what feature writers do all the time, and feature articles are a kind of information writing. If you find your class naturally heading in this direction, you might even consider teaching into feature article writing, though we don't recommend you make that the focus of this last bend. Perhaps you'll simply spend a day teaching that information writers do sometimes angle their writing to forward a position or just conduct a small group on this topic for any writers who have shown inclination toward this kind of writing. So, for example, if you are writing about video games and you feel strongly that these games are particularly beneficial to people, you might create a T-chart that lists a lot more pros than cons—and then work that into your information book. It might look something like this:

Video Games Pros and Cons

Fun!	Can become addictive
Builds hand-eye coordination	Can be violent
Builds problem-solving skills	
Teaches you about the world	
Teaches you to focus	
Makes you smart	
Some give you a physical workout (Nintendo Wii)	
Can be a social activity (games you can play with friends)	

Certainly, you'll teach children to give special attention to the sequence of the information in their writing—not just the order in which each section appears, but also the order in which they lay out information within each section. As students develop sections and paragraphs, remind them to think about how the parts go together. How does one section flow from the previous one? Should one section come before another? Why would this sequence work better? How does a paragraph connect with the other paragraphs around it? Which specific transitional word from the list on the transitions chart (you should have one prominently displayed) represents the relationship between two sentences, two paragraphs, two sections?

As you near the end of the unit, stress how important it is that readers are able to follow a book's train of thought, easily taking in and holding on to information, understanding not just how one sentence (or paragraph, or section, or chapter) connects to the next, but also how the whole book holds together. Readers should be able to recount the most salient points after reading; indeed, to teach people the information they have learned.

As they revise their work, students should also consider the size and scope of the parts of their books. Have they developed each chapter fully, and are chapters more or less the same length? Does each chapter have subtopics with facts and details that flesh these out? Are there parts that feel like outliers—that need to be omitted? If so, is there now a need to elaborate on a section more? Nudge students to consider these questions, both on their own and with partners, so that they problem-solve on their own. Students should consider their openings and conclusions, too, paying attention to how they introduce their topics (Are they clear enough? Do they draw the reader in right away?) and to what thoughts or ideas they leave readers with at the end.

Celebration

For a celebration, you might invite children's family members, another class, or adults from your school community to visit your room and learn from your new class of experts. Perhaps you'll set up sections in the room where different kids can talk off of their books to teach about different kinds of topics—all students who wrote books about a person might meet in one corner, students who wrote about an activity might meet in another corner, and so forth. Or you could come up with another way to celebrate children's writing; perhaps they read their favorite parts out loud and then there's time for a Q&A. You will no doubt have ideas of your own for how to celebrate your class. The important thing is that students feel they have a body of work they've developed and polished that has now made its way into the world.

The Literary Essay

*Equipping Ourselves with the Tools to Write Expository
Texts that Advance an Idea about Literature*

RATIONALE/INTRODUCTION

The fourth-grade book *The Literary Essay: Writing about Fiction* is a unit of study designed to teach students to develop and defend ideas about literature. The unit helps students write literary essays that develop strong interpretive theses about literature, are well organized, use textual evidence efficiently to support a claim, and focus on characters and their traits. They progress from simpler, more straightforward literary essays to those built around more complex theses to compare-and-contrast essays.

The implications for this work are big, and if your state tests measure a child's ability to respond to literature, the stakes are high. It is far easier to write a well-structured, cohesive essay about a topic of personal expertise or interest than about literature. Writing to defend claims about literature requires close reading, attention to literary craft, and the ability to cite and defend relevant textual evidence. For this reason, many of you may decide to expose children to literary essay writing in two separate units, beginning first with this unit (a shorter, more basic introduction to the literary essay) and then moving to *The Literary Essay: Writing about Fiction*.

This unit aims to make reading a more intense, thoughtful experience for children by equipping them with tools they need to write expository essays that advance an idea about a piece of literature. This unit relies on children's prior experience writing personal essays, suggesting they do similar work—only this time, they'll work toward the goal of writing an essay about a text.

MANDATES, TESTS, STANDARDS

The Common Core State Standards emphasize the importance of teaching children to read closely to determine what a text says not only explicitly but also implicitly. That is, by fourth grade, students are expected to draw inferences and develop ideas about a text, citing specific details and examples to support that claim (RL.4.1). Similarly, the standards ask that children learn to analyze and interpret texts, analyzing "how and why individuals, events, or ideas develop and interact over the course of a text" (Anchor Standard R.3).

The Common Core is also clear that students must have the ability to write arguments about topics *and texts* (the expectation of the first Anchor Standard for College and Career Readiness). This unit offers students the chance to strengthen and hone their skills at essay writing; in particular, it will support them in transferring and applying all they have learned in *Boxes and Bullets: Personal and Persuasive Essays* to now write essays about texts. The unit also gives you a chance to shore up the areas in argument writing about which your students are unsure. You will want to have all of your data from across the year at hand to ensure that you are helping students move along a trajectory of work and make progress in large, visible ways.

A SUMMARY OF THE BENDS IN THE ROAD FOR THIS UNIT

In Bend I (Generate Ideas about Literature), you'll teach children that just as essayists pay close attention to their lives, so too do literary essayists pay close attention to texts. Children will select a text from several they are familiar with and generate lots of entries about the text. You will teach them to mine the text for ideas, pulling out a favorite passage or line and explaining why that passage stayed with them after they were finished reading or why it is so powerful or how it relates to the rest of the text as a whole. They will then elaborate on these ideas, expanding their thinking so that you can then channel them to choose one seed idea and write a thesis statement that they can grow into an essay. You will probably want to spend only several days in this bend.

In Bend II (Support and Craft the Arguments), children will gather evidence to support their claims, elaborating on and crafting their arguments. You will scaffold children's work as they draft, revise, and edit their essays, working hard at retelling important moments from the text, angled to support their claim, crafting their introductions and conclusions, categorizing their evidence, and incorporating literary terms. This bend will likely last about a week.

In Bend III (Draft and Revise Essays with Increased Independence), children will draft a second (or third) literary essay, this time doing so with increased independence. You will want to raise the level of your students' work by having them transfer and apply everything they learned in the first two bends of the unit to this new essay. You might decide to spend a shorter or longer amount of time on this bend, depending on how your students did cycling through the first two bends, though we recommend moving quickly, having students flash-draft and then revise on the run before editing and publishing their final piece to great fanfare and celebration.

GETTING READY
Gather Texts

For children to write about reading in this way, you will need to decide which piece(s) of literature your children will study in the unit. If your students are in a reading workshop and talking about the deeper meanings of texts in book clubs or partnerships, you might use literary essays as a way to harvest their interpretations of those books and to cross-pollinate your reading and writing workshops. On the other hand, book club work is not essential to this unit. Your students might write literary essays about a short story or a picture book, perhaps a text they read during writing workshop or that they know from earlier in the year.

In some ways it is easiest for children to write literary essays about a short text such as a short story or a picture book; in other ways this is more difficult. Certainly when youngsters write about a short text, it is easier for them to know that text really well, rereading it several times and mining it in conversations with others. They can also locate evidence easily without spending lots of time finding excerpts. On the other hand, any theory a child might espouse will probably have thinner substantiating support when the text is short. For example, if a child claims that Gabriel, in the three-page story "Spaghetti," by Cynthia Rylant, is lonely, there will be very few bits of evidence the child can draw on to make his case!

You will need to decide whether children will write literary essays about short texts they have read during writing workshop or about longer texts they have read and discussed during reading workshop. For our purposes here, we'll assume they are reading short texts. If you make that choice, we recommend you provide children with a small folder containing four possible texts, letting writers select the one that "speaks" them. Be sure you include two texts that are easy enough for your struggling readers. When writers have choices and can write about topics they care about, the writing is better. In this instance, the writers' first choice is the text; their second choice is what to say about it.

The texts you offer as options should be ones you and your class have studied throughout the year. There is nothing to be gained by introducing unfamiliar ones. Provide stories that are rich, complex, and well crafted enough that they reward close study. Cynthia Rylant's book *Every Living Thing* has some wonderful examples. Eve Bunting's picture books are also very rich. The possibilities are endless. One way to support your struggling readers is to direct these children straightaway to a text you believe will work for them, so that all their work during the earliest days of the unit ends up supporting their final published work. Better readers may take a little time reading and writing about a variety of texts before settling on one. This more circuitous route is fine for writers who can produce volumes of writing easily but less fine for writers who eke out brief texts.

You will also probably select one mentor text for whole-class work, threading this one short story through many minilessons, using your (and the class's) responses to it to show children how people go about reading, thinking, and writing about a story. You'll chart what you do with that story, using words that can apply to any writer and any text, and those charts will remind children of the work they can do with their own stories. Again, one way to support children who struggle is to do some work with the text that you hope they will use as the centerpiece of their inquiries.

34

Anticipate the Trajectory of Your Students' Work throughout the Unit

You will need to decide from the outset how much time you are going to spend in each part of the unit. For example, if you know your students have already studied literary essays focusing on a single text, you may only want to spend two weeks working on the first essay (Bends I and II) and then have children write another quick draft or two in Bend III. However, two weeks may not be enough time to take the first essay all the way through the publishing process, especially if you have noted that your children struggled during the *Boxes and Bullets* unit. In that case, you might make both Bend I and Bend II of this unit full-blown studies of literary essay writing (perhaps dedicating two weeks to the first round of essays and another two weeks to the second round). In any case, we recommend finishing the unit by having your students write a fast draft of a literary essay. This will give you ample data to plan the work you'll need to do in *The Literary Essay: Writing about Fiction* unit.

However you proceed, plan to celebrate the children's achievements at the end of the unit. You might have students lay their first and second literary essays side by side and visit one another's writing, complimenting as they go. Or you might set up a rotating display in the classroom that highlights the books as well as the essays, with the literary essays tucked inside the books about which they were written. You might also give the students' opinions a larger, broader audience by posting the essays on Goodreads.com or another literature blog.

BEND I: GENERATE IDEAS ABOUT LITERATURE

Teach children to collect and develop ideas.

On each of the first few days of the unit, you might decide to demonstrate a way of reading and writing about a story and then invite children to draw from this repertoire of strategies as they work with any text they choose from their packets. You might teach children that just as essayists pay attention to their lives, expecting to generate ideas from this wide-awake attentiveness, so too, literary essayists pay attention to texts. It is particularly effective to teach them that writers can capture an image that stays with them after they finish reading a story and then try to explain why that image is the one that stays and explore how that image fits with the whole story. To help the children linger longer with the beauty of the language of a text, you might teach them that writers can pull out one line or a couple of lines of text and copy them onto a page of a notebook and then write to help them figure out why they found the words so powerful. Again, it will be important for writers to explore how the statement fits into the story as a whole. You might also teach writers that it can pay off to record a turning point in the book and explore how this moment fits into the whole book, or write about how they might live differently if they took the story really seriously. Of course, you will not want to suggest a strategy, show it, and then expect every writer to use that strategy to explore a text. Instead, you will want writers to draw from the toolkit (or reservoir—choose the image that works) of possible strategies, using one, then another, as they see fit.

After a day or two of writing about various stories in various ways, you will want to be sure each student has settled on the text he or she will write about. You will also want to channel children to select bits of their writing and their thinking that seem especially important and begin to elaborate on those ideas. That is, if writers select the text fairly early on, the generating and collecting they do henceforth will all be work that sets them up for their eventual essay. Your next mission is to help them grow and eventually choose between some ideas about the selected text. Writers can look closely at the text they've selected and write "I see . . ." followed by the aspects of the text that stood out, that they noticed. Encourage them to write long about this, extending their observations by using prompts to jump-start their thinking: "The surprising thing about this is . . ." "The important thing about this is . . ." "The thought this gives me is . . ." "I wonder whether . . ."

As your students continue to elaborate, you will want to remind them of the ways they are already familiar with for thinking about characters and the work they do as readers. You might ask them to revisit their sticky notes and notebooks and think about what kinds of ideas they are having about the books they are reading. Similarly, if your students are also participating in a reading workshop, you might have book clubs or partners ask, "What really matters about the book we read? What is worth thinking about?" This may help students understand that the work of writing a literary essay is not brand new. It is simply a more sophisticated way of doing what they are already doing.

One minilesson you might want to consider, regardless of whether your writers are adept at literary essays, is to teach them that essayists know ahead of time that some parts of a story are rich ground for analysis. You will want to point out various places they can look for ideas. Teaching them to consider moments of character change, the lessons characters are learning, and the issues (personal or social) characters are facing will give your writers an entry point into great thinking. Similarly, having students focus on parts of the story—a favorite image, a part that is upsetting or disturbing, the part that most reminds them of their life—will open avenues to other rich ideas.

You might remind children of their personal essay work, when they observed their lives and created "thought patches" in their notebooks: "The thought I have about this is . . ." "This makes me realize that . . ." In this same way, they can pause as they read to observe what is happening to a character and then develop an idea using the same sentence starters. You might teach children that these "thought patches" can be extended, that they can use thought prompts to trigger their thinking. Be aware that children are apt to try to extend their thinking only by providing examples; therefore, you will want to encourage them to linger with their ideas, too. Teach them to record an idea using new words, writing, "That is . . ." or "In other words . . ." and then rephrasing the idea. Teach them to entertain possibilities by completing the prompts "Could it be that . . ." or "Perhaps . . ." or "Some may say that . . ." Words and phrases such as "furthermore," "this connects with," "on the other hand," "but you might ask," "this is true because," or "I am realizing that" can also keep children elaborating on their ideas. If you hope that children will write literary essays in which they articulate the lessons they believe a character learns or name the theme or idea a story teaches, it is important that you provide them with strategies for generating these sorts of ideas.

You might use fantastic "thought patches" generated by some of your students as powerful mentors to help all your writers visualize what it is you are pushing them to do. These entries may also inspire you to create minilessons that spotlight your students' work. You might consider making a mid-workshop teaching point in which you ask the class to analyze what makes the work of one of their classmates shine. This helps them articulate the moves they too should be making in their writing.

Help students write thesis statements and plan boxes and bullets.

Next, you will want to teach children to reread their notebook entries to find seed ideas. You might ask them to look for a seed idea that is central to the story and is provocative. In this unit, a "seed idea" is also, eventually, a thesis statement. You can also help children generate possible thesis statements. Whatever structure a child chooses, you will need to help him or her revise it so that it is a clear thesis—a claim or an idea, not a fact, phrase, or question.

Some of your writers might make a claim about a character or a text and then give reasons for that claim, as they did in their personal essays: "So and so is a good friend because A, B, and above all C." "So and so succeeds because of A, B, and above all C." "This is about so and so, who learns/turns out to be/changes to be/becomes such-and-such by the end." For example, "*Because of Winn-Dixie* is the story of a lonely girl, Opal, who learns that she isn't alone after all. In the beginning of the story, she is lonely, and by the end, the whole town has become populated with people she cares about." Or "'Spaghetti' is the story of a lonely boy, Gabriel, who learns to open himself to love. At the beginning of the story . . ."

Alternatively, as in the personal essay unit, writers may want to write "journey of thought" essays: "At first I thought . . . but now I realize . . ." Students may write, "When I first read [story title], I thought it was about [the external, plot-driven story], but now, rereading it, I realize it is about [the internal story]." Or "Some people think [story title] is about [the external plot], but I think it is really about [the deeper meaning]." This thesis would lead a writer to first write about the plot, the external story, and then write about the theme, the understory.

Other students may want to write a thesis statement like this: "My feelings about [story/character/ theme] are complicated. On the one hand, I think . . . On the other hand, I think . . ." With this structure, students can explore how their feelings or ideas about a story, character, or theme are conflicted. The reader feels more than one thing at the same time. "My feelings about Jeremy in *Those Shoes* are complicated. On the one hand I think he is generous and selfless, and on the other hand I think he cares too much about what others think."

Implicit in all these thesis statements is the plan for the essay. If the statement is "My feelings about such-and-such are complicated," then "On the one hand, I think . . ." and "On the other hand, I think . . ." become the topic sentences for separate paragraphs. If the thesis is "At first I thought . . . then I realized . . ." those elements too set up the separate parts of the essay.

BEND II: SUPPORT AND CRAFT THE ARGUMENTS

Channel students to find evidence.

Once children have planned the boxes and bullets for a literary essay, they will need to collect the information and insights required to build the case. You might decide to encourage each child to make a file for each topic sentence (and each support paragraph). For example, if the child's claim is "Cynthia Rylant's story 'Spaghetti' is the story of a lonely boy who learns from a tiny stray kitten to open himself to love," the child might title one file "Gabriel is a lonely boy" and another "Gabriel learns to open himself to love." Each of these files will become a paragraph (or more) in the final essay. On the other hand, students can work their evidence into their drafts immediately, one paragraph on one page, another paragraph on another page.

You might teach children to gather evidence for each subordinate point by retelling a part of the story that supports their idea, then "unpacking" that part by writing about how it illustrates their idea. If you teach them to do this, you will need to help them angle their retelling so it fits their idea. You will also need to teach writers how to quote from a text and then unpack these quotes by talking about how the quote addresses the relevant big idea. Before this unit is over, you may want to teach children that writers of literary essays use the vocabulary of their trade, incorporating literary terms such as *narrator*, *point of view*, *scenes*, and the like.

Guide students as they put it all together and revise.

There are several alternatives for how you might teach children to take what they have collected and turn it into a cohesive essay draft. First, you'll want to teach children to lay all their evidence before them, determining which stories, quotes, and bits of expository writing best support their ideas. Then, using only what they decide to include, writers can literally construct essays by taping the pieces together. You'll want to teach them to use transitional phrases at the beginning of paragraphs and between examples. This may be something you teach them as they draft or save for a revision minilesson.

Alternatively, you might have children fast-draft their essays. They'll still lay their evidence before them, choosing the best pieces for their essays, but instead of eliminating and taping, they'll reference this evidence as they draft their essays from beginning to end on lined paper.

When teaching children to write introductory/concluding paragraphs, you'll want to remind them that essay writers state their opinions and forecast/sum up their reasons. You might teach them to write an introductory paragraph that includes a tiny summary of the story and then presents the thesis statement. The closing paragraph will probably link the story's message to the writer's own life. It's a good place for a Hallmark moment! ("This story teaches me that I, too . . .") An alternative is to link this story to another story or even to a social issue in the world. Also, as students revise their essays, they will want to read their drafts carefully—most likely with a writing partner—looking for places where there are gaps (in thinking or transitions) and filling those gaps as they revise. You'll also want to study your students' writing in relation to the opinion writing learning progression and note places where their essays are still in need of work. These "needs" become perfect revision strategies!

Finally, of course, you will want to teach your writers a lesson or two about editing their essays. First, you will build on the editing work children have done throughout the year, encouraging students to make smarter and smarter choices about paragraphing, ending punctuation, and the like. This is also a great opportunity to teach verb tense, which often switches during an essay—that is, when children are discussing their thinking, they sometimes use present tense ("Gabriel is lonely"), and when they are retelling they sometimes switch to past tense ("Gabriel saw the cat"). This can be confusing for your struggling writers, and you will want to be prepared to help them make good choices—and understand the choices they are making.

For a celebration of this first round of writing, you might have students share their writing with a small group and write quick compliments to each other. You might also consider making copies of their essays and tucking them into the book baskets in the library. As students go to a bin to pick a book, they can read a bit of their classmates' thinking about the story.

BEND III: DRAFT AND REVISE ESSAYS WITH INCREASED INDEPENDENCE

You will now want to spend a few days cycling your students through a fast version of the literary essay process. If your students did well the first time around, you'll make this bend as independent as possible. Allow children to choose the books they will write about, and remind them of strategies for collecting ideas and evidence by hanging the charts you created earlier in the unit. Encourage students to develop a thesis quickly, moving immediately to the collecting of evidence. In this third bend, you'll want to give them increased choice. Some children will create files again. Others may simply make little booklets (a few sheets of paper stapled together, their thesis on the first sheet, their first reason across the top of the second sheet, their second reason across the top of the next sheet, and so on).

Work to raise the level of the work children are doing. You'll certainly want to teach children to use the opinion checklist to assess themselves. Teach them to note what they've done well and what they still need to work on, and then set goals they can work toward. Remind them to use the various strategies you taught in Bend II, this time with increased autonomy and independence. We recommend keeping this bend rather short; the goal is to usher children *quickly* through the literary essay process. However, if your students struggled significantly in Bends I and II, you might decide to slow down and reteach some of what you introduced a week or two ago. Regardless of the approach, students will end Bend III with a second draft. Plan to both celebrate and reflect on these drafts. If children leave this unit with clear goals in mind for essay writing, they will be well positioned to make a smooth transition into *The Literary Essay: Writing about Fiction*.

Revision

RATIONALE/INTRODUCTION

The Common Core State Standards mention revising and editing as important elements of the writing process. And any time that we ask students to reconsider their work, to pause and read back through and try to lift the level of it, we are in fact helping them work to a higher level of thinking.

Many students view revision as a quick fix in the writing process—a time only to change a word here or add a sentence there. While revision does exist on the word or sentence level, you will want your students, as they become more proficient, to see revision as reworking or revisiting entire parts and, ultimately, the whole of a piece.

This unit will provide your children with a chance to take the time to step back and reflect on what they have done and then dive back into previous work with new vigor, making shapely and significant changes. You will encourage them to look over their entire collection of written work and think about how they can make work they wrote earlier even stronger. This sort of self-reflection, so crucial to Charlotte Danielson's work, increases students' ownership over their own learning. Children will have grown as writers and as people since they wrote some of the pieces from early in the year, and it won't be hard for them to imagine new possibilities for those pieces.

If this unit is coming toward the end of the school year, as we imagine, you can tell children that the purpose of this project is for them to end the year with a collection of finished work that represents their writing for the entire year. This means that children can also have motivation for revision. Now is their chance to show the world all that they have learned to do.

A unit on revision is also a unit on independence. All of your writers will not be doing the exact same kind of revision work. Although the unit will channel students to work for a time revising narrative writing and for a time revising expository writing, within those broad constraints, children will be working in different genres and at different paces. This means that they will need to use their entire repertoire of strategies. Children will need to think about what they need to do individually, not about what the class is doing. They will need to look over their writing and ask, "What is it that I will work on now?" Then, they will need to execute that plan. They will, of course, have the support of your minilessons, charts, and the other writers in the room. However, now more than ever, they will steer their own ships, deciding when to move on to the next piece and when to linger.

Creating a space for this kind of independent work will foster writers who take up their pens at any time of day, look at their writing and the world around them, and then begin a writing journey. This work will support children in creating and following through on writing plans for themselves. You will want to foster this motivation to write and to create writing projects for themselves. As children look ahead into the summer, you will want to set them up to keep their own writing lives going. By teaching students to work independently on projects they select for themselves, you will support the goal of living writerly lives throughout the summer. If you build a community of writers who are excited to take this work on, then you are working toward preventing summer writing loss.

A word about this unit before you proceed. We've included this same unit as an optional unit within the third-grade book, but more than likely, your students will be at a different place in their lives as writers this year. You may well approach the unit by leaning on the broad plans for it but altering the qualities of writing that are taught. Use the unit as a time to reinforce anything your students seem to need as writers. For example, you may see from the checklists that across the board, they need more work on endings, and therefore you might make that an important part of this unit. As always whenever you teach, tailor units that we outline so they support the specific children in your class.

A SUMMARY OF THE BENDS IN THE ROAD FOR THIS UNIT

In Bend I (Rallying Students to Revise and Building Up a Basic Revision Toolkit), you will remind children that revision is a crucial stage of the writing process; revision separates "drafters" from real writers. Students will collect their best pieces of writing from work they have done across the entire year—probably choosing previously published texts (and some entries) that feel worthy of revision—and they will place these in a special revision folder. They will then be reminded of some of the basic and most essential of all revision strategies, such as trimming their writing down to the clearest and strongest words, adding details or examples where elaboration is necessary, and writing with a sense of audience. They'll begin revising many of their selected pieces with these strategies in hand. Plan to spend about a week helping your class to revise up a storm.

In Bend II (Deep Revising within a Community of Writers), students will choose one piece of writing from the folder of "good enough to revise work," and they will revise this one piece of writing in far deeper, more meaningful ways than is usual. They'll do this, in part, by asking, "What is the big thing I am trying to say? What message do I hope readers will take away from this?" Students will develop this core meaning, discarding chunks of text that take away from it and creating new text that adds to it. In this bend, support from a writing community (partnerships and clubs) will scaffold children's individual revision efforts. The second bend will likely last about three days.

In Bend III (Revising Narrative Writing), students will specifically revise one piece of narrative writing they produced earlier in the year, with an emphasis on the qualities of good narrative writing that they have learned. Specifically, they will focus on story arc, pacing, sequence, character development, setting, leads, and endings, and will study mentor narrative texts to find inspiration for revising toward a specific effect. Above all, they will examine their work through a critical, revisionist lens. The bulk of this unit will be spent in this bend, perhaps devoting a week and a half to this work.

In Bend IV (Revising Expository Writing), students will specifically revise one piece of expository writing that they produced earlier in the year. This unit has a special emphasis on structural clarity, paragraphing, sequencing, and following the thread of a unifying thesis statement (in the case of essays) or a heading/subheading (in the case of other informational writing). They will also learn to revise with attention to the use of transitions or linking phrases to connect the thoughts within their writing. This bend is shorter than the previous ones and should only take about two to three days to work through.

In Bend V (Editing and Celebrating), students will consolidate all of their revised pieces and edit these for final publication. The focus will be on revising spelling, mechanics, and punctuation (proofreading their own—and perhaps a neighbor's—work) and then reflecting on what kind of writers they are and what kind of habits they need to build to become more effective. Students will also reflect on their growth and their process from initial drafting to final revision and editing, to take charge of their own future learning and move toward independence. At a final celebration, students will have the opportunity to share their before-and-after pieces with their classmates and even next year's teachers. This celebration doubles as an affirmation of students' work and an informal time to create continuity between grades. This is yet another short bend in the revision road and should only take about two days.

GETTING READY
Gather Mentor Texts for Students

Before you begin the unit, you may want to retrieve mentor texts that you have used across the year and perhaps add to that collection with a few new mentor texts. You will need to have on hand both narrative and expository texts.

Use Additional Professional Texts

There are many useful professional texts on revision. You may want to consult Ralph Fletcher and JoAnn Portalupi's books on revision, *Craft Lessons* and *Nonfiction Craft Lessons*, as well as Georgia Heard's *The Revision Toolbox* (it's not just for poetry). For your own reference, you may also be interested in Roy Peter Clark's *Writing Tools: 50 Essential Strategies for Every Writer* and Don Murray's *The Craft of Revision* or *A Writer Teaches Writing*.

Choose When and How Children Will Publish

Since there are many bends to this unit, you may want to break it up by having a mini-celebration at the end of Bend III, after students have spent significant time working with narratives from earlier in the year. You don't need to make a big affair of this. Perhaps you will set up a revision museum, where students lay out their revised pieces, in all their flap and spider-leg glory, for other children and teachers to see. You could also have children set their mentor texts side by side with their revised drafts, illustrating the crafting techniques that they have incorporated into their own writing.

You may want to use this end of the unit celebration as a time for reflection. Students should be given the opportunity to think about how much they have grown as fourth-grade writers. The original writing and the revised writing, side by side, is tangible evidence of this. You may also want to invite fifth-grade teachers to the celebration, as a sneak peek of the writers who will be gracing their classrooms the following year.

Before students begin any revision work on their selected pieces, you will want to make photocopies and set them aside, to be used at the celebrations.

BEND I: RALLYING STUDENTS TO REVISE AND BUILDING UP A BASIC REVISION TOOLKIT

Some of the best writing comes when you rehash. It's in the retelling of stories that the improvement comes. The reflection comes in the polish. What a person will see, what a person will feel, comes in the polish. When you finish polishing your writing, it forms the image you're trying to create. —Donald Perry

Generate excitement for revision work by teaching students that real writers revise. Immerse them in the revision process.

You'll want to start this unit by recruiting youngsters to become purposeful, independent revisers of their own writing. The tone you set at the very start of the month is important. Remember, it might not be altogether thrilling for children to dig out old pieces of writing and look at them afresh. Don't give them the chance to protest, "But we're done with these!" To offset this possibility, you'll tell them right from the start that this month they'll be doing work that separates the "real writers" from the "first-drafters," that the secret to powerful writing lies in revising, that this is what serious, professional writers do *all the time*. It might be helpful to display what real writers, especially those who children recognize and love, have to say about revision. You may want to share the following quotation from Roald Dahl.

Charlie and the Chocolate Factory took me a terribly long time to write. The first time I did it, I got everything wrong. But the story wasn't good enough. I rewrote it, and rewrote it, and the little tentacles kept shooting out from my head, searching for new ideas, and at last one of them came back with Mr Willy Wonka and his marvelous chocolate factory . . . and then came Charlie . . . and his parents and grandparents . . . and the Golden Tickets . . . and the nasty children, Violet Beauregarde and Veruca Salt and all the rest of them.

Or the following quote by Judy Blume.

I'm a rewriter. That's the part I like best . . . once I have a pile of paper to work with it's like having the pieces of a puzzle. I just have to put the pieces together to make a picture.

Children will have grown as writers from earlier in the year. "The older you will always revise the younger you," you might teach. "That is as true in writing as it is true in life. You are smarter, more mature writers now than when you wrote many of these pieces." In this unit, you will expect children to look at their own earlier work critically and self-assess how they might bring up the level of a piece of writing.

It will help to clarify the gist of revision by modeling the process in a brief, straightforward way. Immerse students in examples of revision by showing them how you revise stories from previous units of study, how past students revised (by showing a sample of a former student's work), and by revising class stories together. If you wrote a class story or two on chart paper or a transparency in the first few units, you can have students join you in revising this using a variety of strategies. You might even place before-and-after revision pieces side by side to demonstrate a clear improvement in quality.

Make sure that this initial modeling is simple and that it offers dramatically visible results. Children need to see that revision is an instantly effective process, that it can make a general word more specific, a rambling sentence more concise, a scattered chain of thoughts more streamlined, an ordinary sentence extraordinary. The purpose, at this early stage in the unit, is not necessarily to have children imitate your revision moves as much as it is to prove the meaningfulness of this unit's important work and to spark their enthusiasm for doing it.

You may want to use the start of this unit to set up a revision center in your room, complete with the tools and materials that will aid in the work that children will be doing in this bend and throughout the unit.

Channel students to reflect on their writing year and decide on pieces they want to move to their revision folders to work with further. Guide them to self-assess their writing and come up with their plans for next steps.

Once you have students on board, you'll want them to reflect on this past year of writing, reading and rereading their own work including previous notebook entries, drafts, and published pieces. You'll also want children to ask themselves, "Which piece do I want to revise?" These can often be the best, most developed pieces, ones that children have invested thought and heart into creating. Note that the least successful writing pieces may not be worth deep revision, even if it seems there is much to revise in them. You can teach children to select pieces that have hidden potential, where meaning is not yet evident but can be clearly developed. "What might this piece be about? Can I bring this meaning out?" are questions to ask when looking at an entry. Or one might ask, "Is the meaning clear? Will the reader understand what I'm trying to show? Is there a way to make this more gripping, more interesting?" Sometimes, rereading a piece will inspire a new thought, a new idea, or a new story, and children might recognize this inspiration right away. "Sometimes a piece of writing literally pops with potential," you'll want to tell them. "You might reread and realize there are some other, new things you want to add. Maybe there are entire paragraphs you want to replace." Children may even begin their revision work by actually writing long in their notebooks about why they want to revise this piece and what they want to change about it.

At this point in the year, students will have cycled through several units in many genres and will have plenty of strategies to turn to. You'll want to haul out the archived genre charts, process charts, and rubrics from units past and display these in your room. The narrative and information checklists, for instance, can be very helpful in enabling children to self-assess, and to articulate and plan the next step. In all of your teaching, but especially in this unit of study, it is critical to help students cumulatively apply what they have learned about the qualities of good writing.

Instruct students to place multiple pieces they select in a special revision folder. Since this is a multi-genre unit, you will want to urge children to pick at least one piece each of narrative and expository writing to work with in later bends. While it is possible to teach generic revision strategies for all genres together (as we do in the first two bends), we have structured this unit so that Bends III and IV separate narrative revision from expository revision. Your students should easily recognize the differences in the way narratives and expository texts are built, and they will benefit from learning revision moves that are specific to each genre. Before students begin any revision work on their selected pieces, you will want to make photocopies and set those aside. When you come to the final unit celebration, you will want students to review these copies side by side with their revised pieces to get a full sense of the work they have accomplished.

Teach general revision strategies that work across genres—decluttering, revising sentence structure, and considering audience.

In this first bend, children may pick up and revise many pieces of writing, regardless of genre. You'll help children build up a basic revision toolkit of the most basic, non-negotiable revision moves that all writers build into their process. The first of these is the removal of "deadwood" from their writing. Some call it tightening, decluttering, paring, simplifying, or hacking and slaying; the process is the same and applies across all genres, for writers of all ages. It requires cutting and discarding the inessential word, sentence, or paragraph. Most, if not all, first drafts contain words that do not add to meaning, that simply take up valuable space. You'll teach children various ways to declutter their paragraphs and sentences. Teach children that one may, in fact, cross out an entire paragraph—even two—after asking, "Is this really necessary?"

Another way to teach decluttering is to demonstrate how a writer can cut out repeated ideas, words, and phrases. You may also demonstrate the replacement of a group of words with a single, precise word. For example, "They walked all the way up to the top of the mountain" could easily be "They *climbed* the mountain." Similarly, "She walked silently, trying not to make a sound with her feet" might easily become "She *tiptoed*." You'll want to explain that, in writing, less can be more. Another way to explain decluttering is to teach children to revise their writing at the word level, taking out redundant words. Demonstrate that many adjectives and adverbs are dispensable, because they repeat the effect of the word they are meant to describe. In the phrases *wet rain, shining sun, tall skyscraper*, the adjectives do no work because rain has never been dry, the sun has never stopped shining, and skyscrapers can't be short. Similarly, *smiled happily* doesn't say much more than *smiled*.

Partnerships can be used to support this work. You might guide partners to read each other's writing, lightly parenthesize a "dispensable" word or idea, and then hand it back for the writer to consider whether the word can actually be dropped from the writing. In *On Writing Well*, William Zinsser describes how he used this process with his graduate students' writing while teaching at Yale. Fourth-graders can do this work just as well, once you demonstrate the effectiveness of this practice and empower them to take their own words seriously.

While revision certainly involves taking the unnecessary "stuff" out of a piece of writing, it can also mean inserting some important parts into our writing. You'll want to show children that revising can mean adding an example or a detail that will make a point or an image more specific for the reader.

Similarly, you can also teach children to revise sentence structures to avoid monotony. Fourth-graders often write an entire paragraph that follows a monotonous series of subject-verb sentences, for example:

I went to the mall with my family. We ate ice cream. My sister spilled some ice cream down the front of her shirt. That was her best shirt so she started bawling.

You'll want children to recognize monotony when they read it. Read out the start of each sentence to demonstrate the pattern that needs to be broken: I-went, we-ate, my sister-spilled, that-was, she-started. Explain that this is the kind of pattern that works like a lullaby, putting readers to sleep. You could teach children to revise in ways that break such monotonous patterns by beginning a few sentences with a verb (action):

Spilling ice-cream down the front of her best shirt upset my sister . . .

46

Or you could teach them to liven up their prose by inserting dialogue.

> "It's ruined! My favorite shirt! Waa . . . ," my sister bawled at the top of her lungs. People turned
> to stare.

Audience is another reason to revise: we revise when we have in mind a particular person or group of people who we know will be reading our work and the effect we want the piece to have on that particular person or group. To instill a very real sense of audience, you might go so far as telling children that all their revised work will go immediately to their new teacher as an introduction to their writing, or you could plan a celebration where they will present their work to the incoming fourth-grade class. You may give children the opportunity to choose an audience for their pieces, either in addition to or instead of the whole-class publishing, thereby letting them decide who they want to read their piece and why.

Prepare your writing center with revision materials, as well as scaffolds for how to use them.

Early in the unit, you'll also want to create a writing center that supports revision by setting out various materials and tools. These might include strips of paper to add sentences and sections into the middle of students' writing, flaps of paper to tape over discarded parts, single sheets of paper to staple onto the end or the middle parts, Post-it notes, tape, staplers, white-out liquid, colored pens, and scissors. You may want to create a chart for the writing center that lists the tools, how they are used, and what revision strategies they support. For example, you might list "strips of paper," and then describe a use of paper strips—to add details. You can describe strategies for how to insert dialogue, internal thinking, or physical description when adding details so that kids know to use them for specific reasons. This will help shift the focus from the strips and toward revision strategies. Invite students to create their own revision tools and spotlight the ones that seem to be working well, sharing them as an example for other students to follow.

BEND II: DEEP REVISING WITHIN A COMMUNITY OF WRITERS

Writers evaluate the purpose behind their pieces before revising. They think about what they want to say to their readers and then use this to guide their revision decisions.

In this bend, children will select a piece or two of writing (in any genre) to revise more deeply. This could be a piece they already worked on in Bend I, but if it is not, you will, of course, expect for them to carry forth all they learned from the first bend about removing deadwood, audience awareness, and so on. In this bend, however, you will teach revision as a means to achieve a far deeper investment with writing. Deep revision involves evaluating the very purpose of a piece of writing, and this can result in substantive changes to the original content. Children (like adult writers) are sometimes so proud of the way that a word or sentence looks on paper, or so impressed by the sheer volume of what they have written, that it can be hard to let go. In this bend, you'll teach youngsters that writers are ruthless with the work that matters most. Real writers don't just trim a word here and add a comma there. They stand back and check: Is it working? Does it all go together? Is it the absolute best it can be?" And then they make big decisions.

In every stage of the writing cycle, purpose is key. This holds true tenfold for revision. In this bend, writers will evaluate the purpose behind a piece of writing. Writers often reread something they've written and ask, "What am I really trying to say?" or "What is the one big thing I want the reader to take away from this?" Often, the writer will see a section that seems to be standing separately or a part that doesn't quite go with the rest. This is a time for decisions: should a writer stick to the original idea that he started with? Or should he allow a tangent to develop into its own—possibly bigger, better, stronger—piece?

The answers to such questions will be far clearer when you model the way you tackle these in your own writing. You'll pick up a simple text that you might have created with the whole class earlier in the year or create a new one especially for the demonstration of this teaching, for example:

> Cats are amazing creatures. The cat family consists of leopards, lions, cheetahs, even jaguars. Did you know that ballet dancers are inspired by the way that cats always land on their feet? It's true. If you throw a cat into the air (though you probably shouldn't) it will always land delicately on its feet. Cats are so graceful. My aunt has the video for a musical called "Cats." My favorite of all is Rum Tum Tugger. He always does the opposite of what is expected of him.

You'll want to model your thinking as you revise this piece. "What is the one big thing I'm trying to say?" you'll ask. "Is this piece about cats—the animals? Or is it about *Cats*—the musical? Those are two separate things. One is an essay and the other is a story about 'a time when.' I'm going to confuse the reader like this." You could show children many ways to proceed from there. "Do I want to make this an all-about cats text? I will have to make a decision and then cross out the part that is irrelevant. I could cross out the all-about and just write longer about the musical and about Rum Tum Tugger, for example." You could then proceed to cross out the discarded part to demonstrate the finality of such a decision.

But you also want to show youngsters that a writer works with several options. "Writers, if I want to keep both parts, I have to show how Rum Tum Tugger connects with my 'all about cats.' Maybe I can add:

> People who keep cats as pets might agree that all cats are like Rum Tum Tugger. They seldom do what their human owners want them to.

You'll want to explain: "Writers, this will still take some work to become smooth. But at least it is no longer two different things. It is an all-about cats text where Rum Tum Tugger becomes an example, a piece of supporting evidence for the fact that cats are stubborn creatures."

You can teach youngsters to think purposefully, envisaging the effect they want to achieve with a piece of writing (perhaps using some other text as a mentor) before jumping into specific craft moves that will help them make the required changes. You might suggest that writers read their work aloud, and they may try first revising by varying their reading tone of voice, then changing the writing to match the tone they like the best. They might even try having their partners read the piece aloud as they listen. These moves will help writers embark on purposeful decisions about what they want to say, the tone they want to use to say it, and the effect they want to have on the reader.

Immerse children in a writing community. Teach them how to use partners and revision clubs as a resource for their revision work.

During this bend, you'll also want to set up ways for youngsters to accept and provide revision support to peers. This unit is a great opportunity to show students that strong revision lies not only in their own solitary processes, but also in the thoughts and feedback of a writing community. You will want to offer students opportunities to share, talk, and revise with others. There are many different ways this might go. You might choose to teach a revision strategy in a minilesson and then send kids off to talk and work with partners on how they could try the day's strategy before independent writing. Kids might discuss places where they could try the day's strategy, work together to make writing plans for the period, or help each other get started. In this case, partners would confer prior to writing as a way of planning for revision. Alternatively, you may teach a revision strategy, send students off to write independently, and then schedule time for partnerships to meet at the workshop's end. You might teach students to share how revision strategies are helping the piece, to share before-and-after versions, or to share their further revision suggestions.

Remind children that they don't need to take all of their partner's suggestions and that a suggestion is a recommendation, a possible way to go, not a command. Ultimately, partners have the opportunity to read and reread their stories together, thinking more deeply about their pieces. The Common Core State Standards expect that by third grade, and certainly by fourth grade, students do not solely rely on teachers for feedback, but also use "support from peers" to revise their writing and move their work through the writing process.

You might want to explore various opportunities for grouping children in this bend and throughout the unit. Oftentimes, you'll take this upon yourself, organizing students who have common needs. For instance, you might form a small group of students who are revising essays, another group of students who are working on a collection of pieces, and another group of students who are using mentor texts to revise. Other times, you'll want to support students in making their own grouping choices. You might encourage them to find partners who are working on similar kinds of pieces or revising using specific strategies. You might have one group of writers who are helping each other resequence their stories, another group that is studying leads, and yet another group that is focused on taking their pieces and rewriting them into a different genre.

Regardless of grouping, give children time at the end of a work session to talk in their partnerships or groups about what they tried, what worked, and with what they're still having trouble. Another way you can support the focus of the group is by requiring that they "workshop" one writer's piece each day: one writer will share his work on Monday, another writer on Tuesday, and so on. This way there is a sense that the whole group will focus on one writer's piece, as well as an understanding that every writer is expected to open up her work to the group.

Groups may want to choose a mentor text in their genre to serve as a guidepost for their revisions and talks about their writing. Children may choose from touchstone texts that you've read as a class, from the narrative checklist if they're in narrative writing, or from other sources that you may have available to them in folders organized by genre. During the first days of group work, children may spend time at the end of the writing workshop reading the mentor text as writers, to construct their own language for what they want to try in their writing, based on their mentor author's work.

BEND III: REVISING NARRATIVE WRITING
Focus on revising narratives using the narrative checklist and general narrative structure.

By now, children should have a clear sense of the revision process. In this bend, you'll teach them to revise *narrative* writing specifically. Ask them each to select a narrative piece from the start of the year to revise. Presumably, they will have written personal narratives if you taught a version of the first alternative unit and fiction, so you can help them to contrast their start-of-the-year personal narratives with their best fiction pieces, asking them to think about what they learned to do as fiction writers that they might be able to use to revise their personal narrative stories, making them much better.

You'll also want to highlight the Narrative Writing Checklist that documents what fourth-graders should already know and be able to do as narrative writers. They can assess their narrative pieces against that checklist and make goals for what they still need to do to make them as strong as possible. You might show students a child's text that matches the fourth-grade narrative standards and one that matches the fifth-grade standards (and the checklists) and challenge them to revise their selected pieces so that they are at least meeting fourth-grade (and possibly fifth-grade) standards.

You might begin by reminding students of the general narrative structure: that time moves across a story arc featuring characters, setting, conflict, climax, resolution, and lesson learned. You'll remind children that a narrator or storyteller's job is to carry the reader through a scene (and into the next if the story contains two scenes) across the arc of the story, showing rather than telling, zooming in at specific parts and moving more quickly over others.

To make your teaching effective, you could introduce an underdeveloped narrative as a demonstration text. That is, you may share a Small Moment story with your students and then, over the course of the bend, revise and develop this story to demonstrate various teaching points. For example, if your teaching is focused on developing the heart of a story, then you could visibly ponder over your own Small Moment story and think aloud each step in a way that reveals to youngsters exactly what kind of decisions might go into developing this heart. "Sometimes, writers realize that the way they wrote something doesn't match what they really intended to say. In narrative writing, this often happens if a scene doesn't quite come alive in full detail for the reader or if the heart of the story doesn't seem important enough."

Another possible revision technique for narrative writing is to think like a movie director and decide where to pan out for a wider view or zoom in on a tiny detail. There may be places where a sweeping view of the whole of a scene might be particularly effective, like looking across the entire lunch room and noticing all the tables crammed with kids laughing and eating, and other places where the close-up of a trembling hand might tell the story best.

Teach students to revise based on common elements that are seen in narrative stories—character, setting, and sequence of events.

You will want to help children refine and polish the most important aspects of their narrative stories. One story element you might help them with is character development. "Writers can revise a character to make that person seem so alive that he or she jumps out of the page," you might teach. "One way to really bring a character to life is to bring that person to the center of the stage and let her start talking. Just as we can tell so much about a person from the way he speaks in real life, we can tell about a character from her choice of words and her mannerisms." Read out loud direct dialogue from classic mentor texts to demonstrate how this helps the reader envisage a character. For example, you could pick up a Beverly Cleary book and read aloud practically any character's words to instill children with a realization of authentic character voices. For example, you might say, "Imagine Dad, when he says, 'Ramona, my grandmother used to have a saying. "First time is funny, second time is silly, third time is a spanking."'" Ask fourth-graders, "What is Dad's mood here?" Or read aloud a few quotes from the mouth of Ramona Quimby herself, that most distinctive of characters.

"Please pass the tommy-toes."
"If I can put butter on my mashed potatoes, why can't I put jelly? I put butter and jelly on toast."
"I am *not* a pest."

Point out that Ramona's voice is recognizably different than Beezus's voice and that the direct words each character uses help a reader imagine each one better than any adjective can! You might have a little fun with your active engagements, inviting one partner to write in the distinctive voice of one or two specific classmates and having the other partner guess who. Suggest that writers come to know a character's quirks and habits the same way that we know our own friends and that writers allow these characters to bring their own distinctive voices to the paper.

Similarly, you might teach students to revise their stories with a particular emphasis on setting. You'll teach that descriptions of setting help situate the story and bring a scene to life for the reader. Explain that events are defined by the time and space in which they occur, that a story moves the reader from scene to scene.

Again, mentor texts are invaluable in demonstrating how the setting provides more than just a passive backdrop for a story, how in fact it sets the very mood of the story. Prompt your writers to ask themselves, "Where does this character live? Where does this story take place?" and to consider setting as more than merely a geographical spot by posing a question like "What is the *culture* of this place?" You might explain this by referring to your own city (an area with which children are familiar) and asking children to ponder how one neighborhood or shopping area can be culturally different from another. Urge them to think, for example, how a small-town grocery store may be different from a gourmet supermarket. You might challenge students to "show" the setting by providing specific details rather than by "telling" the reader about this setting using lazy adjectives. For example, telling the reader that "It was a tiny, cramped room," is not nearly as effective as showing them.

> There was no place to put my feet because every inch of space had been taken up by stacks of books, odd furniture items overflowing with dust-encrusted odds and ends, pencils, yarn, chewed up toys, a broken pair of spectacles . . .

You may teach children to reconsider the sequence of their stories, thinking about where to build suspense, where to start, and where to end and then use revision strategies for resequencing, including cutting and stapling. Adding details is an important part of revision. Children can reread their pieces and think about which parts of pieces are the most important sections, and they can elaborate upon those sections. If children are having a hard time determining the most important part of their stories, they might ask themselves, "Where in my story do I show the biggest feelings or the most important ideas?" For example, a student rereading his story about cooking *arroz con pollo* with Grandma on Saturday could realize that the most important part happened when he and his grandmother smelled something burning. He would then decide to develop this part of the story, adding dialogue and small actions that show his feelings. You can teach strategies for adding more details to the text using strips of paper in the middle of sections. It is important to teach children the reasons for altering a draft, as well as to teach the physical work of revision.

Use mentor authors as models for revision work.

You may also want to teach children to review their leads and endings. Show children that they can try writing a few different versions of any part of their story and then think about which version works best. To write new leads or new endings, children can study familiar mentor texts, or new mentor texts you introduce, naming what the author did that the child might emulate. For example, children might reread the ending of *Fireflies* and recognize that Julie Brinckloe ended her story with a strong feeling. They could then try to write similarly in their own pieces. They might notice that an author began her story by describing the setting and try to write similarly.

Mentor authors will play a large role in this unit as students pore over texts that will help them improve their pieces. You'll want to show students how they can study a published text that resembles what they are trying to produce. You may decide to pull out a few great fiction picture books and help your young writers see how this author crafted the details to bring out the internal journey of the main character. All of this work will support the Common Core State Standards for reading, which require that fourth-graders discuss craft within a specific scene and notice how subsequent scenes build upon each other.

Most importantly, you will want to teach your writers that they must find their own mentor authors, combing through the baskets of your classroom library to find texts that they would like to emulate. While it will help them to watch you point out authorial choices and craft moves, it will create even greater independence if you teach them how to notice great writing on their own. You might suggest that your students read like writers, noticing particular parts that worked well in these published texts and then asking themselves, "How did the author do that? How might that go in my piece? Where could I use that language in my writing?" You can model for students how once you've noticed great writing in another text, you can return to your own draft and revise with that particular lens. Although this will happen in writing workshop, this work supports the Common Core State Standards that call for students to notice author's word choice and discuss the intended meaning and effect.

Coach students to think about their writing from their reader's point of view. Writing partnerships and small groups can help with this work.

As children revisit the narratives they've written, shift them into the perspective of the reader so that they pay attention to parts where the reader will need to envision, predict, or anticipate what happens next. Partnerships might help with this, where children read over friends' writing and point out a part that leaves an unanswered question or a part that feels like it might need further elaboration.

Again, as in the previous bend, you can set children up to work in groups. This provides immediate feedback, support, suggestions, and accountability. Groups can discuss strategies, such as adding the setting by creating movies in their minds, remembering where the characters were and what was around them, and then adding description. By discussing the specific revisions they could make, children are more apt to follow through with what they said. You might choose to showcase strong examples of partner and group work by asking children to gather around a group and listen to its conversation, naming the positive qualities they might replicate in their own partner work.

Celebrate the work thus far with a revision museum.

There are many bends in the road of this unit, and by now, your students have spent significant time revising their narratives. This would be a good time to stage a mini-celebration. This should not be anything grand; save that for your end of the unit celebration. One possible way for students to publish their writing could be to have a revision museum. Students can set out their revised narratives side by side with the photocopies you made of the original narratives. If there was a particular mentor author that they emulated, a specific page in a mentor text that highlights a crafting technique that they replicated in their own writing, the mentor book could also lie side by side with their writing. Give the class an opportunity to take a museum walk, chatting with each other about what they are noticing and about how much more powerful their revised writing has become.

BEND IV: REVISING EXPOSITORY WRITING

When revising teaching texts, writers evaluate their texts for clarity and expository structure.

The chance to revisit some of the essays and informational writing that they've produced throughout the year can actually be an extremely valuable learning experience. No longer are children collecting and sifting through miscellaneous information or their own thoughts about a topic. No longer are they researching or trying to teach. A revisionist stance can actually free children to stand back and look at the expository texts that they've already created to evaluate their overall structure and effectiveness.

You'll want to urge your writers to step into the shoes of their readers and try to experience their own writing from a distance. Remind them that the first question that a reader asks is "What is this text trying to teach me?" Writers will want to evaluate their own texts for clarity. One way to be very clear for the reader is to follow a predictable expository structure. Ask children to identify the expository structure that their writing follows. Is it boxes and bullets? Is it cause and effect? Will the structure be easy for the reader to identify?

While revising structure, expository writers will also want to ask:

- Is there a clear theme that threads throughout the essay or section?
- Does each paragraph have a distinct topic sentence?
- Do the subsequent sentences in this paragraph match this topic sentence?
- Do paragraphs connect logically with each other to create a flow?

A checklist such as this can also guide partnership work, where students swap essays to evaluate the structural clarity of each other's expository writing.

Once students have strengthened their paragraphs, you will also push them toward revising in ways that make the linkages between these paragraphs clear. You'll remind them of the use of transitions or linking words to connect one paragraph to the next. It may be easier to do this if writers focus on the topic sentence of each paragraph and decide how these topic sentences connect with each other. You'll also want students to evaluate their headings and subheadings and to see if more of these need to be created.

Teach students to consider the needs of their readers, as well as what they are trying to teach, when making revision decisions.

Then, there are other revision questions: does the reader have ample support to understand technical words (possibly from an explanation within the paragraph itself or through a text feature such as a glossary, sidebar, or footnote)? Would the text benefit from the addition of a text feature? If some of your students have returned to their angled all-about books, you may highlight pages of a great nonfiction book that uses diagrams with zoomed-in images to teach the reader even more. Or, with a small group of students, you may point out how the author starts with the most important information first and then gives more specific details later on the page.

Sometimes, writers realize that the way they wrote something doesn't match what they really intended to say. In essay writing, this can happen if the thesis statement is not clear or is not supported throughout the essay. In other forms of informational writing, this can happen if the heading or subheading does not match the text that follows.

Essay writers may have new evidence to support their ideas from earlier in the year; or they may have shifted their thinking about the subject and need to modify their thesis.

BEND V: EDITING AND CELEBRATING

Allow students to reflect on their own editing needs across pieces, creating personal editing checklists.

Across the year, you've encouraged students to give tricky words their best try and move on, to use spelling patterns from word study to spell tricky words, and to use the word wall to learn commonly misspelled high-frequency words. You've nudged kids to use big fancy vocabulary even when they aren't sure of the exact spelling, and you've been studying words during word study, read-aloud, and other times of the day.

Now is the time of year to bring it all together. Dust off all the old charts—if you've still got them—and teach kids to use them all, all the time. In this unit, you may want to teach kids that they can create their own personal editing checklists by looking across their own writing to notice the kinds of things for which they need reminders. Writers notice their own spelling challenges so that they can always be on the lookout. Anybody who writes knows their own weaknesses. Teach kids to search their writing to see if they are the kind of writer who misspells certain high-frequency words every time. Or maybe they are the kind of writer who always forgets a particular spelling pattern, or perhaps they forget to reread their writing to check it over. Teach kids that every writer has some habit or even a bunch of habits or patterns in his or her writing. Finding those patterns and knowing to double-check for them is incredibly useful.

Celebrate the Writing in the Classroom, as Well as the Writers

As the year and the unit wind down, you will want to take time to have children celebrate the work they have produced and the great strides they have made as writers during this month and across the year. That is to say, you will want to hold a writing celebration that is about not only the writing but also the writers.

If you made photocopies of the original pieces that children revised, you might choose this time to take those pieces out and put them side by side with the newest version. As children share the before-and-after pieces of writing, they can take their classmates on their journey of revision, sharing what made them decide to revise this particular piece, or these particular pieces, and how they chose to revise those pieces. Then too, writers might share how this process enhanced not only their work but themselves as writers.

Prompt students to think about carrying their writing work forward. Invite fifth-grade teachers to share in the celebration.

Many times our children leave our classrooms strong and energetic writers and then return from summer break the following September out of practice and out of passion. If this is the final writing unit of the year, you may want to spend some time helping the kids make plans for how they will take all they've learned with them into *next year's* writing workshop. You might ask children to write a reflection, sharing what they learned and how they have grown. This reflection, accompanied by the original work, drafts created during revision, and the published pieces, can travel with them into next year's classrooms. Next year's teachers might even begin their writing workshops with children sharing their body of revised work and all that they know about writing with the class as a way of building a writing community and learning about the children in their room.

Then, too, you might choose to invite next year's teachers to your classroom during this time to acquaint themselves with the students with whom they will work in the next grade level. These teachers might join your class for a writing workshop and watch them engaged in the process. They can talk with your children about their process and their pieces. They might study their notebooks and folders. They might also join the celebration, partaking in the end-of-year reflection. Listening to your kids share all that they know about writing will help those teachers plan units of study that build on the work you and your students have done.

Poetry Anthologies
Writing, Thinking, and Seeing More

INTRODUCTION/RATIONALE

A poetry unit is an exciting time in the writing workshop. No other genre grants young writers quite the same freedom to experiment with space on the page, to savor the sound of the words they are writing, and above all, to make universal meaning out of close observations, thoughts and questions about the world, and personal experience. A poetry unit of study ushers your students into a new world of making meaning: a world that fosters deep connections between reading and writing and a commitment to repeated revision. This year, your poetry unit could also emphasize collecting poems around a particular theme or topic as a way to push students to write more, think more deeply, and explore various points of view. Writing interrelated poems is more complex work than writing poems that do not connect to one another. In this way, too, this work is more sophisticated than poetry work of previous years.

This unit offers a unique opportunity to zoom in on craft from both the reader's and the writer's perspective. Although poets, like all authors, write to find and communicate meaning, they engage the reader in the surface of the language, the way words look on the page and sound to the ear, more than many writers of prose do. As your kids try out a number of poems on a chosen topic or theme, they will have a chance to experience firsthand how differently crafted texts can offer truly different perspectives on the same subject.

In this unit, you'll invite children to write poems in response to the topics and themes that surround them: poems about finding and losing friends, the power of sports to heal and to devastate. You'll teach children to find the poems that are hiding in the details of their lives. You'll do all this not just because poetry is its own powerful genre but also because the habits children develop as poets—specificity, comparative thinking, understatement, and hyperbole—will serve them well when writing any genre.

Watch for your English language learners to flourish in this unit. Poetry is relatively flexible in terms of grammar, and more can be communicated with fewer words than within the conventions of prose. This often makes poetry more accessible to writers learning

English. Then too, their familiarity with one or more other languages gives them a wider array of grammatical structures, cadences, words, and sounds to draw from as they create their poetry. Expect that *all* your children will bring their own voices to the poems they will create in your room this month, and be ready to celebrate these voices when you see them emerge. Expect too that, whatever the format of publication, every child will draft, revise, and edit several poems, using mentor texts and your lessons as guides throughout the process.

An understanding of poetry from the inside out will help students build a lasting mental framework for how poetry works and support their ability to read poetry with comprehension and craft appreciation, skills that are expected by the Common Core State Standards and the National Assessment of Educational Progress.

You'll want to take this unit as an opportunity to teach the work called for by the Common Core State Standards in reading. For instance, in looking closely at anthologies that include poems from different points of view, your students will also be practicing fourth-grade-level compare and contrast. Then too, the Common Core State Standards expect that our young readers will develop their understanding and appreciation of not only what the author of a text is saying but also how that text gets that meaning across. A unit on poetry also helps students internalize the structural elements of poems (e.g., verse, rhythm, meter), thus preparing them to explain and analyze the major differences between poems, drama, and prose.

A SUMMARY OF THE BENDS IN THE ROAD FOR THIS UNIT

In Bend I (Create a Class Anthology), you will spend several days creating a class anthology around a common theme, in this way demonstrating ways to take on different perspectives and approaches within the same topic. This will set the tone for the students' own work, teaching them that anthologies can be created with a mission to explore a topic from a number of points of view, through different kinds of poetry.

In Bend II (Generate Ideas for Anthologies and Collect Poems), you will spend a few more days helping kids gather ideas for their own anthologies and try out some poems to go with those topics. You will teach children ways to select poems for an anthology and ways to revise toward the bigger theme, perhaps writing new poems to round out their ideas or frameworks. During this generating stage, you will most likely introduce a few strategies for first-try poetry. Then, in a mid-workshop teaching point or share, you'll quickly show how poets don't wait for revision, that any first try is open for rethinking and reworking. Using published poems as mentors during this bend will help you maintain a sense of exploration and inspiration as your young poets strive to mimic the work of published authors.

In Bend III (Get Strong Drafts Going and Revise All Along), you will continue to emphasize the fact that drafting and revising go hand in hand. Children will continue to write new poems but will also spend time revisiting and revising. You'll encourage children to zoom in on a small collection of poems on which to apply revision strategies (these will later become their anthologies). You will teach them to turn prose into poetry by focusing on structure and to revise to bring out the intended meaning of each poem.

In Bend IV (Edit Poems and Assemble Anthologies for Publication), you will spend some days coaching children on ways to prepare for publication. In addition to editing, this may mean creating illustrations to go with the central images of the poems they've written or rehearsing reading their poems aloud in a way that makes their meaning clear to the audience. Children will also refine their work in ways that are appropriate to the form of publication you've chosen.

GETTING READY
Gather Texts

To start off the unit, you'll want to create an environment in which children read, hear, and speak poetry. Perhaps you'll bring in baskets of fresh new poems, poetry books, and poetry anthologies for your classroom library. You will need to have many examples of different kinds of poems on hand! You might recruit the school librarian to help students find, read, and reread poems they love. Don't forget your public library. Try to find anthologies that are focused on a common topic or theme, such as *This Place I Know: Poems of Comfort*, edited by Georgia Heard; *Extra Innings: Baseball Poems*, by Lee Bennett Hopkins; or *If You're Not Here, Please Raise Your Hand: Poems about School*, by Kalli Dakos. Or you might find anthologies that are focused on a science subject, such as *Fine Feathered Friends*, by Jane Yolen (Yolen has written many anthologies that focus on a specific element in nature), or on a social studies subject, such as *Roots and Blues: A Celebration*, by Arnold Adoff. If you do not have many of these books, you will need to create a few folders of connected poems (you might enlist kids to help you with this). If you teach in a Spanish-English bilingual classroom or if you have many Spanish-speaking students, you may want to include some Spanish-English anthologies, and there are many lovely examples; *Gathering the Sun*, by Alma Flor Ada, and *Laughing Tomatoes and Other Spring Poems/Jitomates Risueños y Otros Poemas de Primavera*, by Francisco X. Alarcón, are just two. You may want to explore The Poetry Foundation, an independent literary organization whose website (www.poetryfoundation.org) includes a children's poetry section and honors a new children's poet laureate every two years. A more extensive list of poetry resources is included on the TCRWP website.

Immersion will play a larger role in this unit than in other writing units, from the very start of the unit and all the way through. Because you will want to teach your kids to read poems well and thoughtfully, in addition to teaching them how to use those poems as mentors, you will want to pick some touchstones that serve both purposes well.

You'll also want to make use of the many wonderful professional texts available. These texts will help you imagine the possibilities for the work students will do and the ways you can best support their growth in this important genre. Here are a few professional texts we recommend:

Awakening the Heart: Exploring Poetry in Elementary and Middle School, by Georgia Heard

A Note Slipped Under the Door: Teaching from Poems We Love, by Nick Flynn and Shirley McPhillips

Handbook of Poetic Forms, edited by Ron Padgett

Wham! It's a Poetry Jam: Discovering Performance Poetry, by Sara Holbrook

A Kick in the Head: An Everyday Guide to Poetic Forms, edited by Paul B. Janeczko

Getting the Knack: 20 Poetry Writing Exercises, by Stephen Dunning and William Stafford

Choose When and How Children Will Publish

Where, for whom, and in what format will children publish their poetry? How will they celebrate? This will, in part, be based on what you discover after conducting an on-demand assessment; your decision will also be based on what's realistic for the time you have carved out and your access to materials and publishing/ performance space. As the unit approaches its end, you may invite your poets to make choices about how they will share their poems with others. In some classrooms, students choose to decorate and post their poems in public places around the school and neighborhood. Other classes invite parents and schoolmates to join in a poetry slam, where children read and perform their poems aloud. Other classes may choose to simply compile their poems into an anthology and place it in the classroom or school library.

BEND I: CREATE A CLASS ANTHOLOGY

You'll begin this unit by creating a class anthology of poems around a topic of common interest, all in a few days of quick drafting and revision. On the first day of the unit, you might read aloud *This Is Just to Say: Poems of Apology and Forgiveness*, by Joyce Sidman. In this fictional story, a class of sixth-graders write poems of apology and forgiveness after their teacher reads them the poem "This Is Just to Say," by William Carlos Williams, and then create their own anthology. After reading a few poems from the book, you might say, "We could try something just like this!" As a class you would then quickly brainstorm some possible topics or themes for the class anthology.

You might show how a topic can have several embedded themes: baseball, for example, might include themes like "it's hard to let your team down," "practice makes perfect," and "sometimes no matter how hard you try, you still don't win." Then enlist students to write poems that get at these different themes. You'll need to spend a little time coming to consensus around a topic, then make sure children all have picked themes or messages they want to try out. It doesn't matter if there is overlap: more than one writer can take up the same theme! One poet might choose to write several poems about one theme. Another might choose to write one poem about how "practice makes perfect" and another poem about how "sometimes no matter how hard you try, you still don't win." The logistics are not as important as making sure that students write, write, write. Ultimately, the point of this work is to give students practice using poetry to get across meaning.

You'll want to plan three or four minilessons to teach in this bend. To model the strategies, you might choose one of the themes and write in front of children, letting them inside the process of your writing. You might model zooming in on small moments and vivid images that are tied to the meaning you hope to convey. You might teach children a few of the ways poets use line breaks—to show shifts in time or setting, for dramatic effect, or to influence the way a reader reads the poem. Then, too, you might teach your young poets that they can use all they know about narrative writing when they write poetry. That is to say, poets use dialogue, internal thinking, descriptive details, and other craft moves to bring out what a poem is really about. You'll want to emphasize that the qualities of good writing span genres.

Surround your writers with mentor texts, not just by lining the bookshelves with popular poetry anthologies but by displaying poems around the room—perhaps even having a Poem of the Day display that keeps changing. Mid-workshop teaching points would be well spent delving into some of these texts and sharing how two very different poems about the same topic—"Dreams," by Langston Hughes, and "Listen to the Mustn'ts," by Shel Silverstein, for example—get at different sides of the topic. Hughes's poem is dark and suggests that without our imagination, we are lost; Silverstein is more hopeful, letting the reader know that dreaming is always possible, even when others are naysayers. You can teach students to consider who the speaker might be in each of these poems and what we can tell about the speaker from the ideas that come through in the poem. It's also a good time to teach students that the poet and the speaker may or may not be the same person: that poets can take on the voice or "persona" of someone else. Invite them to try this in their own poems as well.

BEND II: GENERATE IDEAS FOR ANTHOLOGIES AND COLLECT POEMS

During the next week or so, you will want to teach students ways to come up with topics for their individual anthologies and help them write poems exploring different perspectives on those topics.

The generating process is as diverse as poetry itself. Poems can grow out of observations or emotions, out of memories and images, or from a clever turn of phrase that is borrowed, overheard, or invented out of the blue. Poems may grow out of or respond to other poems. They may grow out of a story or stem from the writer's concern about an issue or need to make a difference. As with personal narrative, you won't want to inundate your children with these strategies. Instead, introduce three or four as you teach writers how to use their notebooks as a place to begin collecting ideas and poems. You'll want the choice of theme to feel deliberate and intentional and be one about which the children have some strong feelings or investment.

Continue to look at poems together and give your kids time to wander in the poetry books and anthologies that are in your room. Often, reading poetry with a partner (first aloud, then silently) and discussing it can spark conversations that will lead to fast and furious writing of original poems. You may model how a mentor poem can lead to a poem about the same topic, a poem that follows the same structure, or a poem that talks back to the original poem.

You will want to select a variety of poems to share with the whole class, so that you do not reinforce your kids' ideas that poetry has to look or sound a certain way. Choose a selection of poems from a couple of anthologies that showcase different effects a group of poems can have: for example, a Jack Prelutsky book may include poems loosely connected by humor, whereas Lee Bennett Hopkins's baseball collection has a more explicit topical connection with more diversity of emotion and style. In addition to these touchstones, of course, you will need a much broader selection of poetry books and folders of poetry that students can read independently and use as models.

Combing through previous notebook entries may evoke inspiration. "Flipping through the pages of our previous writing might lead us to poems that are hiding in the words, waiting to be written," you might say, urging your young poets to pry previous notebook entries apart with a pencil, to circle or copy out a line or a paragraph they might turn into a poem. You will remind them that writers return to the same themes again and again and that perusing old entries through this lens should engender some "aha" moments and ideas for new work: "I'm always writing about being disappointed in my brother. Maybe I could write an anthology with poems that get at all the ways I'm feeling about him, to see if I can come up with more than those disappointed feelings."

Looking at images or going on observation walks (in a park or nature preserve, in the community, in the building) with notebook and pen in hand is another way for children to observe and imagine what they might write about. Teach them to first write long about what they see, what they notice, and what this makes them think. Above all, you will try to teach—and model—a thoughtfulness and a wakefulness that is essential to getting a poem going. Nothing you say need be very poetic or profound as long as you uninhibitedly model a sense of being alert to the visual details around you.

Many teachers have successfully started a poetry unit by bringing in song lyrics and inviting children to bring in the (appropriate) lyrics to music they are obsessed with. This is a way both to notice how songs actually are poems (including line breaks, repetition, figurative language, and rhyme schemes) and to inspire new writing based on the lyrics' theme or image. You might share a pair of mismatched love songs ("Love Hurts" and "Love Is All You Need") as a way to show how different songwriters angle their work to give different meanings. Just as some poems originate in ideas and images, some begin, quite literally, with words. A catchy phrase or a lyrical line can play in a poet's head and eventually spur a bigger idea.

You will expect your writers, after a day or two of generating or collecting, to end up with lots of small blurbs and/or first tries, all waiting to become better-crafted poems. Often, these kinds of gathering entries may not start out looking like poems, instead taking the shape of small paragraphs, perhaps like story blurbs for narratives or small patches of thought for essays. This is fine—and to be expected. These entries are initial fodder for powerful poems; they will not arrive in final and perfected form. It's also fine if children are using line breaks and creating entries that *do* look poetic right away. What is important is that children learn to generate ideas that have power and resonance for them.

During the generating stage, you will most likely introduce a few strategies for first-try poetry, then in a mid-workshop teaching point or share, quickly show how poets don't wait for revision, that any first try is open for rethinking and reworking. You may then choose to teach a generating lesson that shows how a first try can spawn new thinking that leads to the writing of a whole new poem, not just changing a word here and there—a new poem that perhaps offers a slightly different perspective on the same topic. In this way you will continue to support an important trend in your writing workshop: writing with volume, which in poetry probably means writing lots of poems and lots of versions of poems rather than writing long poems.

In a mid-workshop teaching point or a share during these first couple of days you could already introduce the idea of on-the-run revision in poetry. You might teach students that poets don't wait until it's "time to revise" to rethink and recraft. You might use an in-process poem of your own. For example, right away I can look at these lines I just wrote about a fight I had with my brother,

> He was so mad
> he threw a shoe
> into the basement wall.
> I was scared of his anger
> as usual.

and add an image from the setting or a detail about an object or piece of clothing that will make the poem more piercing. Poets especially look for a surprising detail or one that adds a new emotion to the poem. You might remind children how in personal narrative, in fiction, in information writing—in every kind of writing—they worked on bringing in important details. Poetry is no different. In this case, I might demonstrate, closing my eyes, picturing the hole in the wall in our basement, and adding some lines.

> He was so mad
> he threw a shoe
> into the basement wall.
> The shoe thumped to the ground,
> leaving a hole, ragged and dark
> between my brother and me.
> I was scared of his anger
> as usual.

Let your students know that as the unit progresses, they will need to go back and collect more entries so that they can write more poems. They need to do this because as their ideas for their anthologies start to shift, they'll need new poems to fill out their ideas. For example, if I'm writing about the troubles of having a brother, I might now need a poem from his perspective or maybe from my mom's perspective (or even the wall's perspective!), and I'll have to write those.

BEND III: GET STRONG DRAFTS GOING AND REVISE ALL ALONG

Early on, you might also encourage children to talk with their partners and write reflectively about the entries they have collected in their notebooks. Children may reflect by writing or saying, "I'm writing about this because . . ." or "I want my reader to feel or think . . ." or "One thing that may be missing here is . . ." This work helps children uncover the deeper meaning in their entries and begin to plan for a collection of poems that shows different sides of their chosen topics or themes.

Now that students have several short entries chock full of meaningful moments, observations, and ideas, you can invite them to draft these more formally and experiment with the craft of poets. You will probably emphasize free verse at the beginning. Rhyming well is a precise skill that many adult poets find difficult to master! Teach children to aim first for meaning and for finding a way to describe what matters with words that will make the reader see the world in a brand-new way. You will want to teach students how to draft the bare bones, the preliminary sketch, of a poem out of the ideas they've generated.

Help students turn prose into poetry by focusing on structure.

Model for students how to mold poems from previous notebook entries or other writing generated in prose. "Poets know how to turn prose into poetry," you might say, showing them that they can discover rhythm in the sentences they've jotted by breaking them up. For example, you might put one of the blurbs you've written up on chart paper or a document camera and read it aloud.

> I was running in the park with my friends, and we were all running together at first. But because I had allergies, I had trouble keeping up with them. Soon I was all by myself, watching my friends run farther away from me. I felt so weak and alone.

"This is not a poem," you'll tell kids, "but I can make it a poem by breaking it into lines. When I take a sentence and stop part way through and write the rest on the next line, I am making what poets call a *line break*." You might continue, "Let's look at my entry about running and make it into a poem by adding line breaks. Wherever I want to put a line break, I am going to insert a little slash. I'm going to add a few and then ask you and your partner to help me." You might turn back to the chart and begin adding, all the while thinking out loud, "'I was running in the park.' That sounds like a good line. I'll break there."

> I was running in the park/with my friends,/and we were all running together at first./ But because I had allergies,/I had trouble keeping up with them.

You would then ask students to help you add other line breaks into your poem, reminding them how mentor poems you've read helped you make choices about line breaks. You might explain, "I know from the poems I've read that sometimes lines breaks go where there are end marks, sometimes they go after important words, and sometimes poets use line breaks just where they think it sounds good to pause." Next, show your class how you can quickly rewrite a draft of your poem, going to a new line at each slash mark.

> I was running in the park
> with my friends
> and we were all running together at first.
> But because I had allergies,
> I had trouble keeping up with them.

Beginning with structural changes to their prose pieces will help students very quickly see their potential as poets. Experimenting with making lines and stanzas will quickly create the visual look of a poem. From there, you will decide which kinds of work to demonstrate for the whole class and which make for good small-group work or individual conferences.

You might also choose to demonstrate for the whole class how cutting lines, or cutting and pasting lines in a different order, can change the tone of a poem. Poets eliminate extra words or repeated ideas and get right to the important stuff.

Instead of:

> I was running in the park/with my friends/and we were all running together at first.

Try:

> We were all running together/at first.

Or, in your model poem, you might show how more syllables in a line can give a breathless, fast-paced feeling, so you might choose that for a line that has a lot of action or where there is a rushed feeling.

> In the park we were all running together at first

But you might add more frequent line breaks—and end up with shorter lines with fewer syllables—in a part of the poem that is quieter or where you want the reader to go more slowly.

> My breathing got harder and
> I started to fall
> behind.
> Soon
> I was
> alone.

As you teach kids how playing with the length of a line affects how poets read their work, you might touch on the idea of meter. Meter—the number of beats/syllables in a given line, plus the pattern of those syllables—will likely be a new or still shaky concept for students in third and fourth grade, but using and understanding poetic devices is something valued by the CCSS.

Poets convey their ideas visually, and children can decide how long or short to make their lines on the page, whether there are stanzas and how many, which words are capitalized, and what kinds of punctuation to use. Children will learn how poets use the white space around the words to pause, take a breath, and make something stand out from all the other words.

Teach students to revise for meaning and create anthologies with a range of perspectives.

Once children have a few strong drafts going, you'll want to teach them poetic techniques for revision and craft moves that will amplify the messages in their poems (and support Common Core requirements for understanding poetic terminology). Their goal will be to create a collection of poems with different tones and perspectives. Drafting a poem or two of your own in front of the class will allow you to demonstrate revision strategies. Aim for children to see clearly what you did, to understand how they might do the same, and also to appreciate how this move made your poem better.

You might begin by channeling your writers to recall revision strategies they *already know* from their earlier narrative and even essay units. For example, they could try starting right in the moment instead of summarizing everything about their subject. They could try being more precise about their choice of words. You'll want to teach your students that poets, like story writers, convey meaning through imagery (you might recall writing using comparisons, tucking in the term *simile*), but that they also convey meaning through the sounds of words. Poets can express their thoughts and feelings through the way they make a line *sound*. They might choose harsh, plosive sounds or smooth, sibilant sounds. Their lines might have rhymes between them or even within them. You might show students published poets who are really skilled at rhyming, like Jack Prelutsky, and teach them that to rhyme is a choice, not a requirement, of poetry. Children might be surprised when you point out that choosing *which* words in a poem will rhyme is an important decision. Your poets might also revise for sound by thinking carefully about the choices they have made about repetition.

Another powerful revision strategy students might recall from what they know about reading poems is to consider how the ending of a poem impacts its meaning. Remind your poets that the last moments of a poem are a gift to the reader and usually leave a special image in the reader's mind or reveal the poet's main idea or perspective. A poet may reread her poem and decide on either a fitting last line or a last line that turns the tables on the rest of the poem. Just like in narrative and essay writing, young poets will want to try out various ways their poems could end.

The list of revision strategies you might potentially direct your poets toward is long, and children will no doubt take to writing poetry in varying ways. To help boost their independence, you'll want to remind your poets to apply their revision strategies to all the poems in their anthologies. Tone and word choice, for example, are work for not just one but all their poems. And since they are trying to create a range of perspectives and tones for their collections, it will be important to use the same or similar strategies toward different goals. If in one poem a child is trying to find as many harsh words as possible to get across how abrasive his brother's anger can be ("he cracked his G.I. Joe against the Jeep"), in a different poem, when remembering that same brother as the little kid he used to protect, he might search for soft-sounding words instead ("the breeze swept soft ringlets of hair into his eyes").

Partner work will be important to keep energy up during revision; you might have partners help each other by giving feedback and even recommending next steps. Your young poets won't be able to contain the urge to read their poems aloud, and partners can either listen or, better yet, read the poem back to the poet to see whether the words sound the way the poet hoped they would. Partners can also notice where there may be holes in a poet's plan for an anthology. In an anthology about school, a partner might note that all the poems seem to be from girls' perspectives—couldn't the poet try a poem in the voice of a boy? In other words, partners can coach each other to try out the teaching you've already done.

As students meet with their partners to read and revise their poetry collections, you will want to urge them to play with punctuation. They might refer to inquiry charts on punctuation. You also want students to challenge one another on the true meaning of their poems. If they want the mood of the poem to be sad, they might decide that it is best to have fewer exclamation points. For example, you might say, "Exclamation points make everything sound upbeat and exciting; they won't fit here," and suggest they add more periods and perhaps a dash to show long pauses. Students might plan to use commas to break apart a list of things or to add more detail-supplying words to their lines: "The bright, yellow leaf died as it drifted, softly, quietly to the ground."

Finally, revision is a perfect time, if you choose, to look at a few standard forms of poetry. Once students have lived with their notebook entries for some time, you might invite them to experiment with how a haiku or pantoum, say, might enhance what they are trying to say and make it feel really powerful and purposeful. Choosing to work on form near the end of the unit, not the beginning, means that students are making *choices* about how and when to use different forms rather than simply filling in blanks to get the right number of syllables.

BEND IV: EDIT POEMS AND ASSEMBLE ANTHOLOGIES FOR PUBLICATION

Teaching students to look for rules of standard English when editing poetry can be tricky, because children's mentor poems might break these rules. It's important, therefore, to help your poets understand that while poetry can break rules, poetry also makes its own new rules—and that's what makes it extra fun sometimes. Just as you probably stressed in relation to their narrative writing, you will want to teach your poets to edit with their readers in mind. Poets make purposeful choices about grammar, spelling, and punctuation, and then they stick to those rules. For instance, a young poet might decide to go to a new line at the end of every idea instead of using a period. When she edits, she will check that she always does this. Another writer might choose to capitalize following standard rules and will check for this.

Children will probably read their poems aloud several times to make sure they sound just right. Again, they should focus on helping their readers understand what they want to say by checking that they have used all the punctuation marks, lines breaks, and kinds of words they need to make their poem sound just as they intended.

As your poets assemble their anthologies, they might need support choosing which poems to publish. Channel your writers to think about subjects around which they might group their poems, or ask them to select the kinds of poems they like best. Children might also decide to include the mentor poems they used or other published poems that fit within their theme. You might even invite your students to create anthologies that are not solely poems. The world of literature is full of texts that blend poetry with other genres. For example, books like *Out of the Dust*, by Karen Hesse, and *Amber Was Brave, Essie Was Smart*, by Vera B. Williams, tell stories through poems. Still other books, like *Toad by the Road*, by Joanna Ryder; Joyce Sidman's *Dark Emperor and Other Poems of the Night*; and the Yolen and Adoff examples mentioned earlier mix poems with informational text. Your poets might cling closely to a mentor anthology and write and revise other kinds of text to accompany the poems they have included.

You will want to support your writers in deciding on an order for the poems in their anthologies as well. Children might return to mentor anthologies at this point, taking a close look at how poems are organized, and pausing to consider, "What if this poem was in a different place? What would the effect be of reading it earlier or later than the surrounding poems?" Then partners can have similar conversations about their own work, coming to final decisions about placement only after having reflected and reconsidered.

As the unit approaches celebration, you may invite your poets to make choices about how they will share their anthologies with others. In some classrooms this takes the form of decorating and posting poems in public places throughout the school and neighborhood. In addition to publishing the anthologies, you may want to consider incorporating a performance aspect to your celebration; students might pick a poem they have written and/or a favorite mentor poem to memorize and perform during the celebration. Poetry is multisensory: create a celebration that reflects the many dimensions of poetry.

As you prepare for the celebration, keep in mind that when you have students illustrating or decorating their work, it's especially important that you teach these activities; simply making drawings for the sake of sprucing up an anthology ranks low in Webb's Depth of Knowledge hierarchy. You can push students to use higher levels of thinking if, for example, you teach them to consider how visuals can either support the tone of the poem or offer another lens, or how the decisions they make about which poems get placed next to one another can change the way the reader will approach them.

This might also be a good opportunity to invite students to carry some of their biggest discoveries about themselves as writers into different genres. A writer might go back to an entry from, say, September or October that fits within her theme and revise it, considering not only the meaning but also the sound of the sentences. An excerpt could find its way into her anthology.

Historical Fiction
Tackling Complex Texts

INTRODUCTION/RATIONALE

There are many reasons to teach a writing unit in historical fiction. Perhaps the most obvious is that students will jump at the chance to write in this particular genre, which features characters that experience momentous, world-changing events like the Boston Tea Party and the Civil Rights Movement. It's no secret that when students are passionate about a subject, they will give it their all, which increases their chances of being successful. Then, too, this unit stands on the shoulders of all the narrative work you've done this year. The opportunity to return to a genre benefits writers enormously, because it means drawing on old strategies with greater finesse and working with greater control. Familiarity with the genre also means that students have the freedom and know-how to transfer and apply all they've learned about narrative craft to accomplish their own goals. Finally, this unit gives children yet another opportunity to move toward mastery of the ambitious narrative goals set forth by the Common Core State Standards.

You'll note that this unit is extremely ambitious. It asks students to write not one but two historical fiction stories, taking both stories through the entire writing process. Meanwhile, it assumes some knowledge of the historical era. You may, of course, alter the plan by scaling it back so students write only one story. The downside of that is they often revisit major revision, so the total amount of productivity becomes limited.

It will be important to think about how you'll support the content related to this unit. That is, it will be difficult for a child to write an accurate and compelling piece about the Boston Tea Party if he or she knows nothing about the event or time period. We suggest you channel all your students to write about a period you have already studied in social studies. This ensures a basic knowledge of the time, and students can quickly reference social studies materials if they need additional information or facts. You can also read aloud historical fiction set in that same time period. Students will learn to take in these texts through the lens of a writer, considering the craft moves an author has made or the elements the author has selected to include. You'll want to be sure that the writing workshop is primarily a time for writing, not a time for researching content or reading historical fiction novels. We suggest you put together a shelf (or basket) of resources children can quickly refer to, as needed, but that you limit the amount of time they spend doing so, emphasizing that they instead spend the bulk of their time crafting stories based on what they already know about the time period in which their work will be set—and on their own best resource: imagination.

A SUMMARY OF THE BENDS IN THE ROAD FOR THIS UNIT

In Bend I (Collect, Select, and Develop Story Ideas), students will recall what they have learned about strong narrative writing and learn a few strategies for collecting and developing possible historical fiction ideas. They will then spend a little time planning and rehearsing, writing in their notebooks in ways that set them up for drafting. As they do this work, they will have on hand samples of historical fiction and other resources related to the time period in which their stories are set. This bend, while short (three days), is ambitious; the writing children produce should be ample and well crafted.

In Bend II (Choose a First Seed Idea and Take It through the Writing Process), students will choose a seed idea to develop into their first full story. They will use timelines and storybooks to try out different ways their stories might go. They will then begin drafting, with an eye on strong narrative craft and on historical accuracy and detail. As they draft, students will pay attention to creating historically accurate plotlines and believable characters and to the elements of narrative writing they have learned, especially storytelling, not summarizing. They will then learn a variety of strategies to revise and edit.

In Bend III (Take a Second Seed Idea through the Writing Process, with Greater Attention to Bringing Out Historical Accuracy and Meaning), students will pick a second seed idea to turn into a full story. Again, they will rehearse for writing, trying out different leads and imagining ways their stories might go. Then they will draft the stories, keeping in mind all that they learned from the first stories they wrote and aiming to write and revise with even greater attention to strong narrative craft, historical accuracy, writing the internal and external story, and bringing out meaning. They will ask themselves, "What do I hope my reader learns from this story?" and "What message or lesson do I want to convey?"

In Bend IV (Edit and Publish: Prepare the Historical Fiction Story for Readers), students will select one of their stories to revise and edit for publication. They will focus on important conventions cited in the Common Core Language Standards, based especially on what you determine the class most needs.

GETTING READY

Gather Texts

It is essential that your students know at least a bit about the historical period in which their stories are set, so it's best that the period be one they have studied in social studies. You might consider reading aloud a book about the time period or showing short video clips to remind them of what they learned. For instance, you might read aloud *Freedom Summer*, by Deborah Wiles, if students are focusing on segregation, or *Pink and Say*, by Patricia Polacco, if they are focusing on the Civil War. Many teachers follow this course of action and it works quite well. Bear in mind that students do not need to know every intricacy about a time period to write a great story about it! You might also consider setting up a basket full of resources on the historical time period children are writing about—pull picture books, images, maps, and anything else you have for children to look at for inspiration and guidance.

The Reading and Writing Project website (www.readingandwritingproject.com) has lists of period-specific titles compiled by teachers throughout the country. For example, around the Civil Rights Movement, you might put together a read-aloud collection of *Goin' Someplace Special* (McKissack), *The Other Side* (Woodson), *Freedom on the Menu: The Greensboro Sit-Ins* (Weatherford), and *The Bat Boy and His Violin* (Curtis). You might also want to read aloud some nonfiction material related to the time period featured. Even if your nonfiction materials are few, you could compile a folder of articles and photos from the time period and create a one-page fact sheet on important people, issues, places, and events for students to refer to. As you compile these materials, keep an eye on length. Shorter texts will be more helpful as quick references than dense books will. It's important that students see these resources as guides to use as fact and accuracy checks, rather than as materials for in-depth research. They won't be spending more than a few minutes at a time with them.

Assessing Narrative Writing

You will likely find it invaluable to start the unit either by looking over your students' most recent narrative writing pieces or with a quick on-demand writing assessment that will help you make teaching decisions about the unit in general. Be sure to also review the fiction stories your students wrote during the earlier fiction unit and conduct an on-demand assessment so that you approach the unit with a clear sense of what your students have mastered and what they need to learn to do. Although your students will be a diverse group, some having more skill as writers, some having less, you'll probably also find that there are some things you will have taught many of them to be able to do and other things that few have learned—yet. Because students will be willing to work with great zeal in this unit, this is a terrific opportunity for skill development. Teacher after teacher who have taught this unit have remarked on the high levels of engagement and productivity they saw among their writers. They also saw enormous jumps in their students' craft and independence.

Choose When and How Children Will Publish

Over the course of this unit, children will go through the writing process at least twice. They will revise each story they write both on the go and at the end of each draft and will then select from these their best piece to prepare for publication. They will each take the piece they select through an extensive round of revision and editing. Part of the preparation for publication will include making sure the story conveys the author's intended meaning and that it maintains the feeling and accuracy of the historical period in which it is set. To celebrate, you might have a gathering during which children dress up as their favorite characters and take on those personas, or you might create a museum exhibit filled with artifacts that children referenced in their stories and ask each child to share information about his or her artifacts. There are many interesting ways you might celebrate a unit in historical fiction writing. Whatever you decide, make it grand!

BEND I: COLLECT, SELECT, AND DEVELOP STORY IDEAS

There are many ways you might launch this unit to help children generate and rehearse ideas for historical fiction. We suggest you spend just a few days in this bend (certainly no more than a week) before asking children to fast-draft their first versions of their stories. Teachers who have taught historical fiction in the past have tried an array of methods; the following suggestions are a handful of ways to generate and develop ideas. We suggest you pick just one or two and get children to do this step of the work quickly. As soon as they have landed on a few ideas, they can begin rehearsing several pages of writing a day, including story blurbs, different leads and endings, and a few one-page scenes. Plan to give children just three to five days to collect, select, and develop ideas before they go off and draft.

No matter what idea-generating strategies you select, you will want to do two important things on the first day. The first is to convey to children that historical fiction draws on the same skills and strategies for strong narrative writing that they have learned and developed this year (and in prior years). You might then quickly review some of those skills and perhaps suggest that the children make goals for themselves of which ones to develop during this unit.

The second thing you'll want to do is convey to children what, exactly, makes historical fiction different from realistic fiction or personal narrative. Say something like, "We've written many kinds of stories before, but historical fiction will be new to us. Historical fiction is an interesting genre because it has so much to do with time and place. In realistic fiction, the setting might be a school, and the author assumes you know what the school is like, but in historical fiction, the author has to describe the place more carefully because she can't assume her readers will know what a school in, say, Colonial America, was like. So all of you will need to think carefully about how to introduce your readers not only to the characters and events in your story but also to the place and time period. For the next few weeks, we are going to write stories situated in a place we now know something about." Fill in a time period your class has studied during social studies. "But even though you all know some important things about this time period, you can't assume that your reader does. So one important job each of you has is to bring that world to life in the stories you tell." You may want to have some historical fiction picture books on hand for children to browse for a quick feel for the genre. You'll also probably read some historical fiction aloud.

Teach children to generate ideas for stories through research.

If you choose this path, you'll want to convey to your students that fiction writers have some important work to do before they start writing. Fiction writers begin by considering lots of possible story ideas, and then, once they have the gist of an idea that they want to tell, they think deeply about the setting, the characters, and the various ways the story might be spun. When situating a story in a historical era, rehearsal is all the more essential. Historical fiction writers need to ask not just "What would make a great story?" but "What might have occurred within that particular time and that place that might make a great story?"

To answer this question, students may need to conduct a bit of research on the historical era in which their story will be set. It is important to remember that this is a writing unit and not a reading unit, so hold yourself (and your children) to quick, cursory research. As children refresh their memories about the time period (doing a little reading or looking at pictures or maps from the time period), they might ask, "What possible story ideas are hidden here?" Teach them to pay attention especially to the issues that matter to the people who lived during that time and to the fabric of daily life—to the transportation, the clothes, the meals, the setting. They will certainly need to learn facts about the time and place, including the issues or aspects of life that catch their attention, but the important work will be thinking deeply about what it was like for people to live through these events, to live in that time and place. Students will read, writing notebook in hand, asking, "What was going on around people who lived during this time period that might be worth writing about?" This means reading responsively, letting even the littlest facts spark empathy and imagination and envisioning. Remind your class that a fiction writer's notebook includes lots of little blurbs about how possible stories could go.

Teach children to generate ideas by thinking of one's own desires and problems.

Students might also collect possible story ideas by thinking of their own lives and how their particular desires and problems (pressure from parents, fitting in, sibling problems, and so on) might have played out during the time period during which their story will be set. Alternatively, they could study photographs or artwork from the period and imagine storylines for the images they are seeing. They might listen to music from the time period, touch artifacts, pore over primary documents, and think, "What stories are hidden here?"

Teach children to generate ideas by considering historical contexts: examine timelines and facts for possible conflicts, characters, and plots.

As you reintroduce children to the time period they studied during social studies, consider using videos as a way to help children generate ideas. For example, if the class studied the American Revolution, you might show a brief *Schoolhouse Rock!* clip on that time period. Be sure to convey to students that the work the class will do together as they watch the video mirrors what they do as they read nonfiction or historical fiction books. Preface the clip by teaching that writers of historical fiction often create timelines of a period to organize the events in chronological order and then later look back at those timelines to think, "What were some moments of conflict that might become central in a story?" "What stories might be hidden in this sequence of events?" Then pause the video and say, "Hmm. The colonists decided they won't give money to England anymore! I bet there is a story there! Who could a character be in this story? What could be taking place?" Then allow a little time for children to jot down story ideas that the video clip may have inspired.

Whichever idea-generating strategy you select, be sure children don't linger, belaboring this part of the process. The idea is that they quickly come up with a handful of possible story ideas before beginning the more rigorous work of notebook rehearsal. This should look very much like the rehearsal work they do when preparing to write fiction or personal narrative. Children could try out different leads or draft short scenes for each of their story ideas, trying on each idea for size. Encourage them to keep their scenes short and focused. Some teachers suggest that the scenes introduce the setting and the problem. This is a surefire way to keep children from writing rambling entries that don't help them uncover the basic premise of the storyline. As students collect story ideas and write entries around these, remind them of the template they learned in realistic fiction units: "[The character] wants . . . but . . . so . . . ." A quick word of caution: many students want to create adult characters—such as a general in a war. Try to gently steer them away from that impulse. Historical fiction offers enough challenges that trying to write from the perspective of an adult living in an earlier time period often distracts from the important writing skills this unit is designed to develop.

Guide children as they test story ideas and characters for historical accuracy and consider other possibilities.

Once students have collected ideas for stories, they can test those ideas by drawing on all they know about the era and the genre. A writer might reread his or her entries and ask, "Does this make sense for the time period? Does it ring true? What is a different way it could go?" Perhaps a student has jotted in her notebook, "A boy in the Civil War wants to spend time with his older brother but he is working all the time so they drive together to Florida on vacation." After asking herself whether the story makes sense for the period and rings true, the writer could revise the story blurb to say, "A boy in the Civil War wants to spend time with his older brother but their family is divided and he is on the Confederate side, so . . . ." That is, the child would factor in potential period-based motivations and conflicts and delete scenarios that ring true only for current times. Nudge students to think even about details such as time-appropriate names, dress, speech, and interests.

Some writers, meanwhile, will be more wed to historical facts than to story ideas. While you will, of course, celebrate their passion for history, their focus on historical facts may come at the expense of their story-writing skills. Remind these writers that they are first and foremost story writers. You could say, "Writers, when I collect ideas for historical fiction, I want to make sure that I am still writing about people and issues that feel true to me. Remember that when you wrote realistic fiction you learned that you can give the struggles of your own life to a character. You can still do that when writing historical fiction—as long as those struggles don't conflict with the time period." You might then share that one of your biggest challenges is getting along with your older brother. Then help them imagine what that same struggle may have looked like if set in another time and place: "If I want to give this same struggle to a boy who lives during the Civil War, how might that look? Maybe he gets into an argument with his brother. Oh, I know! I learned that young boys weren't supposed to go to war, but some lied about their age and got in anyway, so maybe this boy wants to fight, but his older brother tells him he's too young. Maybe they have an argument and . . ."

Because your students will have already written a fiction story earlier this year, you can give them a quick reminder of the sort of story rehearsal they need to do and then give them time to do it. Be sure the charts from your realistic fiction unit (and personal narrative unit, if you taught it) are front and center, and hold students accountable for doing the strategy work you have taught—in their own way, according to their own time frame. Be ready to teach from whatever good work your students do: "Writers, I want to point out that Keisha isn't postponing revision. She's revising her story blurbs without my even suggesting it, and doing so to make sure they ring true for the time period. Smart work!"

BEND II: CHOOSE A FIRST SEED IDEA AND TAKE IT THROUGH THE WRITING PROCESS

Once children have spent a few days collecting and rehearsing in their notebooks, you will want to channel them to begin drafting their first seed ideas. Children will likely benefit from minilessons that reinforce narrative structure and craft, particularly in relation to historical fiction. Many teachers who have taught this unit successfully have found it helpful to begin by focusing on plot before moving on to character development. One reason for this is that without a clear (manageable) plot in mind, children often tend to set their characters up to do too much over too long a time, with the result that their stories feel unrealistic and unfocused. Rather than writing about a character who learns something meaningful through a single heroic act, children create unlikely sagas that ramble on for pages. Structure, character development, and meaning all suffer.

Facilitate planning and storytelling: create a cohesive, focused plot.

It is important that students settle on a tool to facilitate planning and story-telling the progression (or plot) of their stories. They might use blank story booklets made from folded copy paper or loose-leaf paper. Writers can sketch a micro-sequence of events on the four pages (no more) of their booklets and then touch each page and story-tell that moment to themselves or to a partner. These booklets are fun to make, and students will easily make half a dozen, each representing one possible way the story could unfold. Model with your own story booklet how to bring the whole sequence of sketched events to life by story-telling each page of the booklet. Illustrate the difference between storytelling and summarizing by first telling a detailed and engaging drama for each page of your booklet and then telling each page in summary. Show students how you revise your telling—each time telling it more vividly—to bring out the character's inner thinking more, to make the setting more vivid, to heighten tension.

This part of the writing process is a great time to do a little preemptive work. Before your students begin drafting, you will likely want to gather their most recent plans for their stories and review them for any possible pitfalls. Keep an eye out for stories that contain too many scenes, are not historically accurate, or have structural or other difficulties. You might then quickly meet with students to iron out some of these issues, so that they move toward drafting with the strongest possible story ideas.

To help children think about plot in a more focused way, you might teach them that in historical fiction, often a character is put to some sort of test. Often the test makes the character consider his or her position on something larger happening in the world around him: a war, a movement, a push for new rights for a particular group of people. Put another way, you might teach that in historical fiction, what a character wants/struggles with is often linked to the larger events happening around him or her.

Help students develop believable, interesting characters.

Once writers have begun to settle on a story idea (one that includes a character with some motivations who gets involved in an action/problem/struggle), they can spend some time making their protagonists more real. You might draw on Session 3, "Developing Believable Characters," from *The Arc of Story: Writing Realistic Fiction* to remind writers to develop their characters by thinking about outside traits and inside traits that might go together. As children do this work, coach them to ask again, "Does this ring true for the time period?" To illustrate this, show children how you consider a character from one of your own story ideas: "Let me check my notes again. What would a girl during this time period be wearing? What is apt to be going on around her? And what do I know about this period that could affect how she feels on the inside about the events in my story idea?"

To further develop their characters, students might write flash-drafts of single everyday scenes. The challenge will be for the writer to bring both the character and storyline to life by living in the shoes of the character while that character has dinner with her family or walks to school in the morning. Writing quick everyday scenes will spotlight for students the ways these stories take the shape of any fiction writing and also how they demand crafting that is particular to historical fiction. The flash-draft allows you to assess whether your students remember the instruction from previous narrative units about writing a scene—the importance of including dialogue and small actions, writing the external and the internal story, making a movie in the mind, and story-telling rather than summarizing. These flash-drafts will guide your choice of whole-class minilessons you still need to teach, as well as the small groups you'll lead. Chances are you'll discover that students need lots of help story-telling, not summarizing, which is at the heart of any successful fiction. If so, be sure to revisit all that children learned during the personal narrative Small Moment work. Remind them that their stories should revolve around two or, at most, three small moments.

Likewise, you'll want to be sure that students' casts of characters don't spiral out of control. Your children's short stories will be much more poignant if they focus on just a few characters whose actions, words, and experiences illustrate something powerful, rather than on the inhabitants of the entire town. Limiting the number of characters also lends itself to staying in the scene. A child is much more likely to story-tell when she is writing about a particular family that hid one child during World War II and to summarize when she writes about zillions of families that helped countless people.

Even if students' character development is thin and/or their plots are hazy, resist the urge to linger more in rehearsal, because it is sometimes the urgency and clarity of planning and drafting that crystallize young writers' thinking and nudge them into more accountable, coherent storylines. Bear in mind, too, that children will have ample opportunity to revise their stories, both on the go and once they have completed first drafts. The rehearsal work should take no more than a day or two before children dive into drafting.

Support students as they draft and revise: craft a compelling historical fiction story.

Once students have experimented with ways their stories could go and set up their plans, they will begin drafting. Students may plan to write each of the two or three scenes in their booklets on a new sheet or two of loose-leaf paper. As they begin this work, teach them that historical fiction writers set the scene, choosing details that tell the reader when and where the story takes place. Children might quickly reread the opening scenes from some historical fiction mentor texts, noticing how one author might have both explicitly stated the date while also including period-specific details, as in *The Babe and I* (David Adler), while another author might bring readers into a scene through a character's actions and then layer in period details, as in *The Bat Boy and His Violin* (Gavin Curtis). Students can use these same strategies in their own writing. One writer might start his story, "It all took place in the summer of 1775, the summer when my father went to war, the summer when Boston was divided among Patriots and Loyalists, the summer the British redcoats became our enemies."

As students begin drafting, the most important thing to emphasize is that they story-tell rather than summarize. Ten minutes into their work, pause all your students and teach them to ask, "Am I telling a story that could have happened during the time period, or am I just reporting about the time period?" Summarizing large and important swaths of text, rather than writing inside a moment, bit by bit, is a frequent tendency of writers who are new to this genre, which depends on relaying historical facts to the reader. To help them address this challenge, teach children how to sprinkle historical details by showing, not telling, them here and there, tucking in this information much as they would any other situational matter in a story. Tell them that part of the job of a historical fiction writer is to find ways to get pertinent information across without miring the story in one historical fact after another. Remind children that starting a story with a character saying something and doing something, making sure the action is detailed and specific, will immediately get them to story-tell.

Spend just a little time helping children think through an ending that aptly resolves the main character's problem. Just as they experimented with different possible leads, students might now try out different endings. Encourage them to think about realistic ways their stories might end. Does the character learn a lesson? Change in some way? Steer children away from endings in which an outside force sweeps in and magically fixes the character's problem.

Meanwhile, you'll want to remind students of the narrative writing habits they have been perfecting all year, and continue to keep any charts you developed on qualities of good narrative writing within easy view as children write. Children can then recall that strong narratives include not just the external story but also the internal story (characters' thoughts and feelings), that the pacing of a narrative changes, depending on what's happening, and that the heart of a story is given great attention and detail, so that readers know to slow down and pay attention.

Students should revise and edit as they write and again once they finish their piece. As they revise, they might consider whether the heart of the story is as powerful as it might be, whether all parts of the piece bring out their intended meaning, whether the story events are as clear to the reader as they are to the writer. As they edit, they might review their pieces for conventions, including punctuation, verb tense, preposition use, and order of adjectives.

BEND III: TAKE A SECOND SEED IDEA THROUGH THE WRITING PROCESS, WITH GREATER ATTENTION TO BRINGING OUT HISTORICAL ACCURACY AND MEANING

For children to get the maximum benefit from this unit, it is essential that they go through the process of taking a draft from seed idea to revised draft at least one more time. In this third bend, then, you will want children to quickly thumb through their notebooks to the rehearsal work they did the first week and pick a second idea to develop into a story.

Tell students that they will do everything they did the first time, only this time they will give even greater attention to narrative craft and to writing a story that brings out a particular meaning. Does the character learn a lesson that the reader might learn, too? Does the writer have a particular feeling about this time period that she wants to convey through the character's journey? Now is a good time for your children to think a little more critically about the time period in which their stories are set.

As students begin planning and rehearsing for their second story, you might teach them that in addition to studying information about the events of a period, writers of historical fiction can also collect facts about the details of daily life, social issues, technology, and important places. Students can jot quick facts and ideas, write longer entries about what they imagine and envision, make sketches, and even paste photographs into their notebook. Their research might span a whole range of topics—fashions, modes of transportation, schools, gender roles, and events. Encourage them to (quickly) take note of whatever sparks additional development of their second story idea.

Revisit historical fiction elements with greater attention to historical detail and meaning.

As students begin drafting, you might teach them to consider the setting again, just as they did the first time around. Teach them that historical fiction writers use setting not only to orient readers to the particular time period in which a story is set but also to convey the feelings surrounding a major historical event. If people are living in a time of unrest or having to make do with less food or fewer supplies, the writer might describe the setting in ways that paint it as bleak.

You might also teach children to pay closer attention to how they depict the characters in their stories. One way to do this is through dialogue. Teach them that historical fiction writers use dialogue to convey something about the period in which their characters live. For example, a story might include characters who speak in code to cover a secret operation, such as hiding runaway slaves during the Civil War or Jews during World War II. Historical fiction writers also include dialects particular to time periods. They may also use more formal speech patterns when someone with less power is speaking to someone with greater authority.

On a related note, this is a good time for kids to develop some "expert" vocabulary. Mysteries are full of words such as *perpetrator*, *investigator*, and *red herring*. Fantasy often has archaic, medieval words such as *saddlebags* and *abode*. And historical fiction will be full of historical terms such as *hearth*, *homestead*, and *pinafore*. Your writers can create individual and shared word banks of the technical words they are collecting as they read, and they can weave these into their writing. Using period-specific terminology will lend a greater sense of accuracy to their work.

Channel children to pay attention to story scope and believability.

As you read students' first drafts, you probably found that many of your writers tended toward the melodramatic. Characters got killed dramatically in battle or suffered horrific injuries or rose up like superheroes to defeat the enemy. Whereas in Bend II you may have let the melodrama remain, now you might decide to use it as an opportunity to teach students to revise for believability. A good place to practice this revision is in a scene in which the main character faces a crisis, choice, or problem. You might teach students that in moments like these, a story will ring more true, and also garner readers' sympathy, when characters are believable—that is, when they are flawed or complicated, when they are not all good or all bad, when they falter or make an unexpected alliance with another character or do something that is perhaps out of character. The easiest way for children to learn how to do this, of course, is by basing their characters on people they know or on themselves—that is, on their own observations and reflections. You might model this by saying, "Maybe instead of making my character defeat the British soldiers all by himself, I should think about what could really happen in life. Usually when things get better in our school, it is not just one person who changed everything. For example, when you all decided that our school needed more nonfiction books, you had a schoolwide bake sale to raise money for new titles. Hmm. I wonder whether my character might join forces with just his older brother, and maybe instead of defeating the British soldiers (which after all, feels unrealistic and isn't historically accurate), the two might end up making headway with just a few British soldiers. Maybe they even get through to those soldiers by talking, not fighting."

Additionally, you'll want to spend some time teaching students about integrating setting into their drafts. Encourage students to think broadly about setting. It's not just where the story takes place—the physical location—but also the time period, the mood, and all the historical details, big and small, that are the markers of that setting. What would a home look like in this time period? Would it be different depending on the character's class or role in the culture? What about the landscape? Roads? Weather? Show kids ways that they could include setting as either chunks of description, or else weave it throughout the narrative, or both.

Teach children to revise for historical accuracy.

It is predictable, of course, that your students will need to revise for historical accuracy, so you may write your own draft in such a way that it, too, requires this revision. Then say, "Oops, in my story Polly wrote a letter that only took two days to arrive! But this book about the colonies says that everything took days and days to travel from state to state. I'll have to change that detail in my story." Teach students that historical fiction writers continue researching alongside their writing, aiming to ensure historical accuracy. They look at both their entire draft plan and the specific details they have been developing and ask questions like, "Does this feel true to the time period? Do I know a more specific way to describe this piece of clothing, item in the house, person's name, and so on?" On the other hand, you don't want students to be bogged down by researching each and every fact as they write, so teach them that when they are on a roll in their writing, rather than stopping everything to check a historical fact or detail they're not sure about, they can put in a blank space or another word as a place holder. Then, when they have finished the draft, they can go back and do some quick research to fill in those gaps.

Teach children to craft satisfying endings.

Finally, you can teach your students that historical fiction stories can end without having to resolve the historical struggle. True, one character could potentially work to overcome—and even have great influence within—a particular struggle, but usually one character, especially a fictitious character, will most likely not defeat the entire British army, give women the right to vote, or solve the stock market crisis. Rather, the main character may make some small stride—or not (perhaps the story is simply about her learning something about the world in which she lives and resolving to live according to her own beliefs). Historical fiction tends to highlight something about a particular time period, yes, but it isn't always about making huge strides that change the course of history. In fact, more often than not, it features small acts of bravery (Annemarie delivering the bread and cheese basket with the hidden handkerchief in *Number the Stars*, Mama covering up the names of the kids who once owned her class's "new books" in *Roll of Thunder, Hear My Cry*, or Rose delivering food and companionship to a young Jewish boy in *Rose Blanche*).

Just as students critique a book's ending in a book club discussion, teach them to think equally critically about their own story endings, to consider whether their storylines are tied up, whether they have created a satisfying ending that is also historically accurate. A student who is considering a Superman-type ending like "so maybe in the end Jason can be so worried about his brother that he tells Abraham Lincoln he needs to free the slaves" might instead reveal something the character discovers about himself or about his brother that was hiding there all along: "Maybe Jason learns that while he cannot change what happens to his brother, he will still always remember his brother as the one who believed in him." You could also revise this lesson to include a reflection on your notes about the time period.

BEND IV: EDIT AND PUBLISH: PREPARE THE HISTORICAL FICTION STORY FOR READERS

At the start of the final bend, you will ask students to choose between the two stories they wrote, deciding which they would like to revise and edit for publication. Encourage children to think carefully about which piece both feels stronger and has the potential to grow even more.

Meanwhile, you will make decisions about what types of editing lessons your students need in these final days of the unit, both as a whole class and in small groups. Historical fiction—really any sort of narrative writing—is a perfect opportunity to study how the syntax of the narrator can often be different from that of the characters. Even each character's syntax might be different. *Catching Up on Conventions* (Francois and Zonana) has a powerful section about teaching students code-switching—how different contexts require different forms of grammar or punctuation. Writers could also benefit from the sentence apprenticeship described in *The Power of Grammar* (Ehrenworth and Vinton), in which students lift mentor sentences from a historical fiction book they are reading and try out the syntax and punctuation in their own writing. This aligns with the Common Core language standards.

You might also remind your writers that they already know a great deal about ways to edit their pieces. Perhaps you'll revisit editing checklists or charts you have gathered throughout the year and teach your writers that they can read their piece slowly, look through one lens at a time (more sophisticated writers could probably manage several at a time) as they reread, stopping at each sentence to ask themselves, "Did I do such-and-such correctly in this sentence?" For example, students could pay attention to words they use to describe objects, places, or people and then edit for word choice, researching to see whether there are more historically specific ways to name them. Or they might consider how punctuation changes the sound of characters' voices—short and choppy, long-winded, excitable. They may look for verb tense, checking that they are maintaining that consistently, either using past tense throughout to indicate the historical nature of the events they are describing, or perhaps using present tense to help readers feel they are running right alongside the protagonist. Again, all of this work also supports the Common Core language standards.

Throughout the year students have also learned that giving words their best try as they spell and moving on is of utmost importance, as is using spelling patterns they know from word study and using the word wall to spell and learn commonly misspelled high-frequency words. Continue to encourage students to use what they learned in previous units now, as they head toward publication. As you near the end of this month's unit, you might want to teach children that there are specific strategies partners can use to help each other edit their writing for spelling. For example, you might teach kids that instead of spelling the word for their partner, they can say, "See if you can use one of the spelling patterns from word study to spell that word" or "Do you know a word that sounds like that word? You can use it to spell this one." Kids can even remind each other to look at the entire word on the word wall, not just one letter at a time. Coach kids to use a chart in the room to remember some of the things they can say to each other instead of spelling the words for each other.

You'll also want to teach students that historical fiction writers can read their writing aloud, either to themselves or to their partners, noting how words, punctuation, and other structures help set the mood, tone, and content of their pieces. Students will have already had experience editing through this lens during their work in realistic fiction (see Session 14, "Editing with Various Lenses," in *The Arc of Story: Writing Realistic Fiction*).

At the end of the unit you will be amazed how far your students (and you) have come. Historical fiction is not a simple genre. Through your support and guidance your students will not only have learned to read and write this genre, but they will also have developed a deeper understanding of narrative craft. You will no doubt want to celebrate their accomplishments in grand, public ways. One choice might be to have students dress up as characters from their stories during your celebration, perhaps talking and behaving as the characters would. Another choice might be to have students dramatize brief moments from a few student stories. Or you might invite students to pair their narratives with some of the historical artifacts they collected during the first week of the unit, such as photographs or illustrations, and then showcase these as museum exhibits. Whatever you decide, make this a big deal: "Writers, it's time to celebrate our hard work! Historical fiction writers publish and celebrate in ways that help our readers best get lost in the worlds we've created. And today, you're going to begin getting ready to have that effect on our visitors."

Journalism

INTRODUCTION/RATIONALE

Teachers who have taught this unit report to us with glee the remarkably high engagement of their students, as well as their productivity and increased focus as writers. You could teach a unit on journalism in such a way as to achieve a variety of goals. This particular spin on the unit helps students learn to write information texts quickly, to revise purposefully and swiftly, and to write from positions of thoughtful observation within their community. The unit imagines that you will teach your class first to write concise, focused reports that tell the who, what, where, and when with a sense of drama. A typical news report might feature headlines such as "Spider Gets Loose from Science Lab" or "Tears During Dodgeball."

Later in the unit, you'll support students writing news stories with more independence, helping them get a firm grasp on this, and then you'll up the ante, setting your students up to become involved in deeper investigative journalism projects. Within this portion of the unit, you'll teach them to conduct interviews and collect observation notes, to ask questions, to ponder the meaning of everyday happenings, and to write in ways that suggest significance. Investigative pieces, in contrast to news stories, may have titles such as "Spiders Get a Bum Rap at P.S. 4" or "Dodge Ball Teaches Toughness."

A SUMMARY OF THE BENDS IN THE ROAD FOR THIS UNIT

In Bend I (Generate News Stories), children will learn the basics of journalism writing. They'll learn that journalists observe a newsworthy story and then report on it by telling the "who," "what," "where," and "when." They'll learn the importance of choosing precise details that convey the facts of the story while also hooking the reader, and they'll have a chance to revise their writing, paying attention to word count and word choice and aiming to write lean accounts.

In Bend II (Revise News Stories for Structure and Tone), children will have a chance to write yet more news stories, this time with greater attention to crafting succinct, dramatic pieces. Students will learn about the structure of a news story and how to craft engaging leads comprised of essential information followed by in-depth descriptions of the event. During the revision process, students will fine-tune the officious tone and concise language of their stories.

In Bend III (Cycle with Purpose through a Journalist's Process), students will further hone their skills in writing news stories. They will learn how to conduct interviews to add accuracy, authentic quotes, and balanced reporting to the story. They will practice how to create leads that engage readers and endings that bring closure. In this bend, students will write one to two news stories with greater purpose and skill.

In Bend IV (Edit and Publish), students will work with partners to edit each other's news stories, checking not only for conventions and paragraphing, but also for journalistic structure and content. Small groups might work together to polish headlines and create mini-newspapers, possibly even adding illustrations or photographs, to share with the school in celebration.

GETTING READY
Write and Gather Demonstration Texts

Before beginning this unit, you will probably want to enlist the help of a colleague to create a newsworthy drama in your classroom.

You might also gather news stories that illustrate the features that you plan to highlight in your minilessons: attention-grabbing headlines, leads that convey the essential information. As you select texts, you needn't think about the *topics* of the texts but instead about the *organizational structure* and the tone of the texts. You'll want to choose news stories that resemble those you hope your children will write.

Consider How and When Your Children Will Publish

You will want to consider your options for how children will publish their news stories. One option is to create a mini-newspaper that you can share with other classrooms or the whole school. For a celebration, you might invite another class to join yours and have students share favorite parts of their news stories. You might also consider how to involve students more in the creation of the mini-newspaper. Who will design the layout? How should the news stories be grouped? What about cartoons or other illustrations? There are a variety of ways you could do this, and the main thing to remember is that students should feel that their writing is being sent out into the world to be read by others.

BEND I: GENERATE NEWS STORIES

Stage a drama in the classroom.

One attention-grabbing way to start the unit is to create a scene—to stage a drama—perhaps between yourself and another teacher, designed to provoke a reaction in your students, to get them to sit up, take note, and think, "Now that's newsworthy!" For example, another teacher in the grade might enter your room during read-aloud and begin snooping through your desk. Continue reading, but show signs that you're distracted by her nosing through your stuff. Finally, look up and say, "Do you need help?" Your colleague might respond, "I'm looking for my math book. Did you borrow it and forget to return it?" Assure her that you haven't seen it, and resume reading. The teacher can continue rummaging, and perhaps help herself to your favorite pens, saying, "I'm borrowing your colors because I know you have my math book somewhere." By now, students should be shocked—perhaps even outraged on your behalf.

This is just one possibility. You can figure out your own scenario. One teacher, for instance, became frightened when she "saw" a mouse in the classroom. Another had the principal come in, seize one of the books in the classroom library, and declare that it was banned. The simulation should be short and dramatic, with some kind of physical interaction as well as verbal, so that students can observe (they don't know it isn't real!). The teachers who played out these scenarios used their bodies to show their fear or their hands to show disbelief, and they said things that were quotable, as in "There's a mouse loose in the room . . . could it be in someone's sneakers?" and "Give me that book. These children deserve to read freely!"

This may seem hokey. It may even seem sort of crazy. You can absolutely come up with better plans! You just want a small, sudden, observable drama. What you will find is that staging a confrontation works because the suddenness of the altercation hooks the kids right away. You needn't stage an altercation, of course. You can catch one. School yards and lunch rooms are full of mini-dramas every day.

Channel students to write about the incident.

All of this is a drumroll leading up to you announcing to your kids that as writers, when things happen, they need to think, "I can write about this." Tell them that in instances like this, they can write a news story about what just happened. With a sense of urgency, say, "Open up your notebooks. You have five minutes to write down what you just witnessed." This work needs to be very quick and intense.

To scaffold your more struggling writers, you might say something like, "I, for instance, am thinking my news report could start, 'Today at 8:55 A.M., children in room 506 were startled to see . . .'" If you use a journalistic tone, including third person and a sense of specificity and drama, kids usually pick that tone up right away.

After a few minutes of writing, you might ask students to share with their partners. You might also read aloud some of their reports, telling the class to listen for things other "journalists" did that they feel worked well. They'll usually notice that when people wrote dramatically, this drew in readers. They will appreciate the use of detail, and they'll notice if some of the writing "sounded like" a news report. This entire endeavor can take just a few minutes if you keep the pace brisk: three minutes for the simulation, five minutes to write, ten minutes to share with partners and the whole class. All of this, of course, would depart from the usual minilesson template. Breaking stride is a good thing from time to time.

You may want to extend this early work. If so, you might ask your students to imagine that a newspaper is going to publish their report, but only their first twenty-five words will be published. Therefore, they need to make those first twenty-five words count. They can change the words any way they want or delete some and use other words from later in their story. Give them five minutes to revise just the first twenty-five words, suggesting they aim for more specificity, detail, and/or drama. You will probably want to write these on a chart under the heading "Qualities of Strong News Reports."

Then let them get right to it, heads down, doing immediate revision. Ask them to share again with partners and then at their tables. They could simply read aloud some of the lines they've written that they especially like. It's amazing how, in one day of writing, they'll have learned to observe closely, write quickly, and immediately revise! Their second versions will be better, especially since they only have to work on the first part of the story. They may add a title, and when you teach them to do this, you will be teaching a bit about angle or perspective. Typical titles might include "Kids Jump on Desks," "Fifth-Grader Traps Mouse on the Run; Mouse Seeks Freedom," and so on. You could finish your lesson by starting a word chart of technical and academic words that relate to news reporters, such as *witness, this reporter, incident, bystander,* and *quoted.* You'll keep adding to this list over the course of the unit. Eventually you'll also start a second chart of vivid words: *shocked, bolted, surprised, dismayed, perplexed.*

Channel students to gather notes and generate entries.

That first day is intense and fast-paced, and it will set the tone for the kind of writing children will be doing this month. The next day, your more usual unit of study can begin. Probably the first thing you'll want to teach your young reporters is to generate stories from the world around them. You might recruit students to ponder the questions "What is news?" and "What is newsworthy?" To support this inquiry, you might display several different kinds of news stories and help the class study these to decide what stories make the news. Youngsters can be helped to notice that news must be current: if it's new, it's news. Without taking long to do this, you can help students notice the diversity of issues and subjects that news stories cover so that children realize that news covers famous people, big events, sports matches, the weather, and all sorts of human interest stories. Explain that events are newsworthy if they affect a wide range of people—more so if they're close to home and relevant to the population that is reading about them. If you need to drive home that point, you could show children local as well as global news. The former will feel more accessible to children. The school's annual fundraiser will be easier to cover, for example, than the war in Afghanistan.

Of course, you don't want to cancel students' writing to study journalism. In any unit of study, children need to be writing almost every day for at least half an hour. So if you engage in a bit of a study about journalism, keep in mind that you can do some of this work side by side with the process of generating stories.

For children to be writing up a storm in this unit, you'll need to help them know that there are topics all around, ready to be harvested. Demand that children seek out and report on the stories in the world around them. Did they witness an injustice being committed in the hallway? An argument in the boys' bathroom? A commotion on the playground? An adventure during science lab? A scuffle on the bus? The Pulitzer Prize–winning journalist Donald Murray describes the journalist's job as "writing with information," which requires paying attention to the world, and asking the questions, "What is? What isn't? What should be? What's going on, and what does it mean?" Talk to your journalists about becoming a fly on the wall—observing, listening, taking furtive notes.

You will certainly want your students to be recording entries, and you can decide whether these are in their writer's notebooks or whether you want to create portable writer's notepads for the occasion. There are two reasons to invent portable notepads. First, these can later be deconstructed and taped into writer's notebooks (which therefore also allows the notebooks to stay alive). Then, too, the portable notepads can help journalists assume new roles and walk into the new parts. But it is also possible for children to dust off their writer's notebooks and to use this unit to give those notebooks more life.

Whatever the writing tool may be, you will want to encourage your students to go around the school, looking for incidents that could become the center of a news story. "The best reporters are not born in the middle of war, riots, or conflict. They don't just happen to be passing by as world-changing events explode conveniently right before their eyes," you might tell children. "The best journalists seek out the action, positioning themselves in the spots where news is likely to occur." Explain that news stories are born, for example, when a reporter notices an act of heroism or an injustice, reads something on the bulletin board or overhears the talk near the lockers. Encourage your reporters to seek out the hotspots of action, in school and out, gathering fodder for stories. If you have writing workshop at a time when your students can visit these sites, take the children with you, notepads in hand, and have them come back and write a quick news report, not more than maybe 150 words long. You'll want to have them write several quick stories of this nature—providing time for writing—and then promptly sending them off into the "world" to collect more stories. You can also make "journalists' passes" so students have permission to disperse to other spaces in the school to do this.

Because you'll need your reporters to collect enough information to actually write the story, you'll teach them to take comprehensive notes. "Once they sniff out the makings of a newsworthy story, reporters investigate its details," you might teach. Journalism's conventional formula for getting complete information on a news story involves answering the five Ws and one H.

- What happened?
- Who was involved?
- When did it occur?
- Where did it all take place?
- Why did it happen?
- How did it happen?

That's actually a lot of information. The five Ws and H reflect good old-fashioned common sense that is as relevant and crucial to teach today as it ever was. Once you hold children accountable to answering this list of questions in their stories, you'll see that this is far from simple. Your reporters will need practice, and they'll benefit from studying mentor texts. You may start by modeling how to identify the five Ws and H answered in the headlines and leads of several mentor news stories until students can pick these out quickly and independently. Have partnerships support each other in this work. Midway through their writing, you might encourage partners to swap stories and find answers to the five Ws and H in each other's stories.

As writers create and gather investigative notes, remind them of Roy Peter Clark's advice from *Writing Tools*: Don't return to the writing desk without the "name of the dog." In other words, teach reporters to procure specific details that will help make the story come to life for readers. If their story is about the healthier cafeteria menu, for example, it will be helpful to mention that a sleek bottle of balsamic vinaigrette now stands in the spot that used to house the mayo tub. If the story is about an after-school skateboarding contest, a mention of the orange flame streaking across a purple board will help bring the story to life. Urge them to collect a quote—the direct words that somebody said—and to jot these with accuracy, along with the source.

Coach your reporters into producing three to four small news stories in this beginning bend and accept that these will be far from perfect. At this point, you will want your reporters to practice finding a newsworthy event to write about, to gather information on this, and to put it down on paper. Don't balk at the prospect of rushing students through this process. Issue deadlines, by all means. They are an essential elements of journalism. In *Writing to Deadline*, Donald Murray shares on this topic: "When I give talks, people ask, 'How do you get the writing done?' My answer, 'I have a deadline.' But they ask, 'How do you know a piece of writing is finished?' 'When I get to the deadline.'" Murray goes on to describe how, early on in his career as a journalist, he wrote dozens of stories to deadline during his eight-hour shift, describing it as intensive training. You can think of this bend as intensive training in the art of generating news stories for your students. Practice, not perfection, is the aim of training.

Once youngsters have completed three to four quick cycles of gathering notes on a newsworthy event and fashioned these into rudimentary stories, you'll slow this pace and bring up the level of their news report writing skills by teaching them to revise. As they look over their stories to revise, you'll want to tuck in teaching that helps them learn the journalist's craft.

BEND II: REVISE NEWS STORIES FOR STRUCTURE AND TONE

Journalism is an increasingly wide field of writing, and there are many places to begin when teaching the journalist's craft. It makes sense, however, to start with structure. Because the technique, structure, style, and purpose of journalism are distinct from other forms of informational writing, children will need explicit instruction on how news reports are put together.

Teach students to craft a lead.

"A news report is like an upside-down pyramid," you might say, drawing this basic shape to explain. "The entire lot of basic information comes first," you'll say, pointing to the widest, top part of the inverted pyramid. Explain that journalists position the most substantial, interesting, and crucial information at the very start of the story so that the reader's most basic questions are answered within the very first sentence or two. Unlike fiction, the "lead" of a news story cannot afford to tantalize the reader with the promise of a mystery or entertain with witty dialogue; instead, it must provide hard facts with lucid briskness. You might begin this bend on "craft" by asking reporters to look back over the stories they generated in the first bend and to revise the leads to those stories. Share several mentor texts and point out that all the five Ws are usually answered within the headline and the first sentence or two. You might even lift several good news leads from various newspapers and post these around the room as examples, urging students to identify specific information provided. Set your reporters up to mimic this top-heavy structure that presents the biggest and most important information first. That is, teach them to revise the leads to their news stories so they position the answers to the five Ws within the very first sentence.

Demonstrating this process will be invaluable. You might take a collected class experience and develop the lead of a news report from it, for example, "Students at P.S. 4 were shocked this Monday morning to find that a mouse had gotten loose in their classroom."

Point out that a simple, single sentence, like the one above, can provide the reader with immediate information on who, where, when, and what. Draw students' attention to the fact that a news story is not necessarily written in the chronology of how an event occurred. Unlike a story, it does not begin, "The day dawned bright and beautiful. Not a cloud in the sky, and the creek next to the factory bubbled cheerily. There was no warning that aggressive rioting would disrupt the streets by noon." Instead, a news report begins straight from the time, scene, and reasons of the big news itself: "Student riots rocked the campus of Wiley University, starting Friday after the last classes, protesting against . . ." News stories give the reader the big information first. There is no build-up to a climax, unlike texts with typical narrative structures.

Guide students as they move down the remainder of the inverted pyramid.

You'll go on to teach students that this lead is usually followed by a more detailed description of the event, supported by background information. This often includes a narration of the sequence in which something happened, pointing out what happened first, what happened next, and so on. You'll encourage your reporters to revise by adding details of what affected people or witnesses said, for example:

"I am outraged," said one parent. "My daughter could have been bitten."

Explain that reporters strive for balance, doing their best to cover two sides of every story. One way to do this is to document what a variety of witnesses said or felt or what two different sides feel about an incident. To the above quote, therefore, a reporter might add:

Some students, however, expressed concern for the safety of the mouse. "It is a harmless enough creature and has as much right to life as any of us," declared one concerned fourth-grader. "I hope this doesn't bring out the traps and the poison."

You will want to help students note the use of the word *however* in the sentence above, explaining that a reporter will often say, "Some people think this. However, others think this." Remind children to use a news reporter's tone, using people's full names when writing about them and referring to them by their last names if they are referred to again in the same piece. Since this is revision work and your reporters are no longer at the "scene" (time and place) of the actual story, they may not have all the ready-made quotes or details at their disposal; you can bend the rules and allow them to invent these if needed.

You'll also want to help students revise the endings to their news stories. You'll explain that the inverted pyramid often ends with the least crucial information—usually with conjectures made by a witness, by an authority, or by reporters themselves. These conjectures or guesses sometimes detail the possible effects that an event might have on neighbors or on the future or what follow-up courses of action might be. For example:

A thorough investigation by the Department of Health is likely to be conducted.

Or

Science classes will go on as usual in Room 107, but no student is likely to forget the furry little visitor.

During the revision process, you will also want to draw reporters' attention to the tone of news reports, explaining that this tone is different from the tone used in a memoir or a story. Read aloud a few news reports and ask students to note the use of the "outsider" third person and the officiousness with which facts are reported with accuracy and specificity. You could download a video clip if you want, anything from the famous eye-witness reporting of the *Hindenburg* to a news clip or a sports clip from the night before. Help your students talk about the tone of the pieces, the role of the reporter and the audience, the rapidity with which information is conveyed, and any language they notice.

Finally, draw students' attention to language. The best news stories are concise, to the point. They don't waste words. Demonstrate how long-winded writing can be tightened, how excess words can be lopped off to crystallize meaning, how a single precise word can replace a phrase. Share news stories in which the journalist has practiced showing, not telling, and make clear that the best news stories contain only those carefully selected details that will evoke a strong sensory reaction in the reader.

The revisions your reporters make to their existing stories should take no more than three or four days, especially since news reports are shorter than many other kinds of writing. You'll want to keep your writers moving, engaged, and challenged by new tasks, moving them along to the next bend.

BEND III: CYCLE WITH PURPOSE THROUGH A JOURNALIST'S PROCESS

If you've ever tried your hand at an ice cream cranking machine you'll have noted that the first cycle is always hardest—that the more cycles you crank through, the quicker and easier they become. This is true of everything, including cycling through a new kind of writing. Your news reporters have come full cycle, generating a news story, gathering information for it, crafting a lead that answers the five Ws, inserting dialogue, and finally, structuring it through to a logical end. Now is the time to let them have another go—expecting that their process will be easier, smoother, more purposeful. In this bend, you'll send them off to find and report on more news.

Some teachers have structured their workshops like actual newsrooms, with students assigned to various topics or parts of the school. For instance, some students may be in charge of stories in the lunchroom, others reporting on bulletins from the main office, others from behind the scenes in the after-school parking lot, and so forth. Turning students into experts on one division of the school will increase their investment in their reporting.

Teach students how to conduct and incorporate interviews.

This time, you can set your reporters up to be more purposeful from the start. You might teach them to interview a witness or key player of the news that they are reporting. Your students will see that interviews provide more than just some "quotes." They also provide important content for the story itself. Teach a simple interview protocol where you model how the reporter establishes a rapport or connection, asks a few preliminary questions, listens carefully for interesting ideas, asks follow-up questions or says, "Say more about that," and elicits specific examples. You might want to conduct some role-playing scenarios with the children so they can practice interviews. Coach them in their body language, their note-taking, and their listening skills. You might conduct a mock interview of a colleague to demonstrate and also have students interview each other to practice. Explain that reporters take care to preserve the direct words of their interviewee to retain accuracy and authentic quotes for their news story. For this reason, reporters take along a small voice-recorder or practice speedy note-taking in shorthand. They may want to bring a partner to help with note-taking when they interview.

"Journalists prepare for interviews." This is important teaching. Students will not necessarily do this unless you prompt them to, and it can dramatically alter the results. Urge students to plan some specific questions to ask, to approach the interview with these questions in hand, and even to anticipate answers and prepare some follow-up questions for the most obvious answers. As they practice interviewing each other in class, make sure they listen carefully to their partners and ask questions that extend or clarify the answers that they receive.

You'll want your reporters to get multiple perspectives on a story so that they learn "balanced" reporting. You might even insist that they conduct more than one interview, that they get more than just one voice represented in their story. So they will interview the shopkeeper as well as the customer, the superintendent and the teacher as well as the student. When they return to the writing desk, demonstrate how to incorporate these direct quotes in a way that strengthens the story. "You don't just reproduce the entire interview verbatim, nor do you put in quote upon quote," you'll teach. You'll want to explain, "Journalists are selective in what they pick to quote. Usually these are the most provocative ideas or the ones that will stir the readers' imagination. They use only the best quotes."

Support students as they craft the news story.

Your journalists already have practice in presenting information hierarchically in the inverted pyramid. This time around, they will draft a purposeful lead that not only presents the most important information head-on but also grabs readers' attention. Explain that a good lead—spelled *lede* in journalism—is always written in the active voice. For example, instead of the passive sentence, "Students were stunned by a mouse scurrying across . . ." the active lede would read, "Mouse stuns students." Similarly, "Experiments were conducted by scientists to . . ." is a passive sentence and needs to be converted to an active lede: "Scientists conducted experiments to . . ." You'll need to let students practice converting passive sentences into active ones, and set partners to check out each other's leads for passive weakness.

Similarly, help students craft endings that provide an element of closure. Granted, the inverted pyramid suggests that the least important information is contained in the ending, but this does not mean that the ending can be shoddy and poorly developed. Instead, a thought-provoking ending leaves the reader thinking more about the news. To decide what to put in an ending, journalists might ask "What background and technical details might the reader need?" You might ask students to look at the endings of several news stories that they've studied in the past month and notice what purpose these endings serve and mimic this in their own writing. Explain that there is nothing more frustrating for the reader than finishing a story with unanswered questions still hanging—that the journalist ensures that he or she has covered all sides and angles before ending.

Crafting an effective headline is part of journalism. The headline is more than a harbinger for the story that follows. It actually has a marketing angle too. "Read it here!" news headlines seem to yell. "You won't believe what just happened in our world. Read on." Ask students to collect a few headlines and study what is similar in many of them, how they are structured and their economical use of words. In particular, draw students' attention to the use of strong verbs in each headline. You'll urge students to craft similar headlines for their own stories, headlines that hook the reader with concise, strong words. Explain that shorter headlines can have more impact than longer ones and demonstrate how a longer headline might be shortened to the bare minimum of words possible.

In this bend, you'll want students to generate only one or two stories but to craft these with purpose and revise them into perfection until they feel ready for publication in the upcoming bend.

BEND IV: EDIT AND PUBLISH

The relationship between the journalist and editor is an interesting one. A newspaper editor is a taskmaster, writing critic, and advisor rolled into one. You might have your journalists become each other's editors and ask them to check each other's writing for the correct use of conventions, paragraphing, and the inverted pyramid structure and to try to answer the five Ws and H within the headline and lead. You might have small groups come together to polish their headlines and arrange their stories together to create mini-newspapers to share around the school.

To bring this process to life, you might even allow students to create cartoons or illustrations or to insert actual photographs to include in their newspapers. If you have time, you might talk a little about photo-journalism and how each photograph in a newspaper supports the story in answering the five Ws and H. Again, mentor photos and illustrations in actual newspapers will play an invaluable role. Celebrate these newspapers by displaying them in a prominent place for the world to admire.

Part Two: Differentiating Instruction for Individuals and Small Groups: If … Then … Conferring Scenarios

THERE IS NO GREATER CHALLENGE, WHEN TEACHING WRITING, than to learn to confer well. And conferring well is a big deal. It matters. If you can pull your chair alongside a child, study what he or she has been doing, listen to the child's own plans, and then figure out a way to spur that youngster on to greater heights, you will always be able to generate minilessons, mid-workshop teaching points, and share sessions that have real-world traction because these are really conferences-made-large.

However, knowing conferring matters doesn't make it easier to master. Even if you know that learning to confer well is important, even if you devote yourself to reading about the art of conferring, you are apt to feel ill-prepared for the challenges that you encounter.

I remember Alexandra, tall with long brown hair and a thick Russian accent. I'd pull up beside her after the minilesson, notebook in hand, ready to execute the perfect conference. We'd talk, I'd research, and without fail, every time, I'd be left with the same terrifying realization: "She's already doing everything! I don't know what to teach her." In an attempt to preserve my own integrity, I'd leave her with a compliment. Despite having joined our class mid-year, despite the challenge of mastering a new language and adapting to a new culture, Alexandra implemented anything and everything I hoped she would as a writer. I thought, "What should she do next?" I was stuck.

Then there was a child I'll call Matthew, who in truth, represents many others across my years as a teacher. It felt as if I was always conferring with him—modeling, pulling him into small groups, implementing all the scaffolds I knew of—and yet he didn't make the progress I hoped for. In reality, it felt like nothing worked. As I'd sit beside him, looking over his work, I couldn't help but wonder what was happening. Why was my teaching passing him over? What do I teach him, right now in this conference, when his writing needs *everything*?

If you have had conferences like these that have left you wondering what's wrong, know that you aren't alone. Teachers across the world find that conferring well is a challenge. Most of us have, at one time or another, written questions on our hands, or on cue cards, that we want to remember to ask. Many of us have mantras that we repeat to ourselves, over and over. "Teach the writer, not the writing." "It's a good conference if the writer leaves, wanting to write." "Your job is to let this child teach you how to help."

Many of the books on conferring will help you understand the architecture of a conference. You'll learn to research first, then to compliment, then to give critical feedback and/or to teach. You'll learn tips about each part of a conference. When researching, follow more than one line of inquiry. If you ask, "What are you working on?" and hear about the child's concerns with one part of the writing, don't jump to teaching that part of the writing until you generate a second line of inquiry—whether it's "What do you plan to do next?" or "How do you feel about this piece?" or "If you were going to revise this, what might you do?" There are similar tips that you'll learn about for other aspects of conferring, too.

But you will no doubt feel as if there is another kind of help that you need. You will probably want help knowing not only *how* to confer, but also knowing *what* to teach.

Visiting hundreds of schools has given me a unique perspective on that question, a perspective that may be difficult to come by when you are in one classroom, with one set of children who have very particular needs. After working in so many schools, with so many youngsters, I've begun to see patterns. I notice that when X is taught, children often need Y or Z. I meet one Matthew in Chicago and another in Tulsa, Oklahoma. I meet Alexandras in Seattle and Shanghai. And I've begun to realize that, despite the uniqueness of each child, there are familiar ways they struggle and predictable ways in which a teacher can help with those struggles. Those ways of helping come from using all we know about learning progressions, writing craft, language development, and grade-specific standards to anticipate and plan for the individualized instruction that students are apt to need.

The charts that follow are designed to help you feel less empty-handed when you confer. I've anticipated some of the most common struggles you will see as you teach narrative, opinion, and information writing through the units of study in this series, and I've named a bit about those struggles in the "If …" column of the charts. When you identify a child (or a group of children) who resembles the "If …" that I describe, then see if perhaps the strategy I suggest might help. That strategy is described in the column titled "After acknowledging what the child is doing well, you might say …" Of course, you will want to use your own language. What I've presented is just one way your teaching might go!

Often you will want to leave the writer with a tangible artifact of your work together. This will ensure that he or she remembers the strategy you've worked on and the next time you meet with the child, it will allow you to look back and see what you taught the last time you worked together. It will be important for you to follow up on whatever the work is that you and the youngster decide upon together. Plan to check back in, asking a quick "How has the work we talked about been going for you? Can you show me where you've tried it?"

Some teachers choose to print the "Leave the writer with …" column onto reams of stickers or label paper (so they can be easily placed in students' notebooks). You also might choose to print them out on plain paper and tape them onto the writer's desk as a reminder.

I hope these charts will help you anticipate, spot, and teach into the challenges your writers face during the independent work portion of your writing workshop. (The charts are also available on the CD-ROM).

Narrative Writing

If ...	After acknowledging what the child is doing well, you might say ...	Leave the writer with ...
Structure and Cohesion		
The story lacks focus. This writer has written a version of a "bed to bed" story, beginning with the start of a day or large event ("I woke up and had breakfast.") and progressing to the end ("I came home. It was a great day."). The event unfolds in a bit-by-bit fashion, with each part of the story receiving equal weight.	You are learning to write more and more, stretching your stories across tons of pages. That's great. But here's the new challenge. Writers need to be able to write a lot and still write a *focused* story. What I mean by this is that writers can write a whole story about an event that only lasted 20 minutes, and it can still be tons of pages long. To write a really fleshed out, well developed, small moment story, it is important to move more slowly through the sequence of the event, and capture the details on the page.	Not the whole trip, the whole day: 20 minutes!! Write with details. I said, I thought, I did.
The story is confusing or seems to be missing important information. This writer has written a story that leaves you lost, unable to picture the moment or understand the full sequence of events. She may have left out information regarding where she was or why something was happening, or may have switched suddenly to a new part of the story without alerting the reader.	I really want to understand this story, but it gets confusing for me. Will you remember that writers need to become readers and to reread their own writing, asking, "Does this make sense? Have I left anything out that my reader might need to know?" Sometimes it is helpful to ask a partner to read your story, as well, and to tell you when the story is making sense (thumbs up) and when it is confusing (thumbs down).	I reread my writing to make it clearer. I ask myself, "Does this make sense? Have I left anything out that my reader might need to know?" If I need to, I add more information or a part that is missing into the story.
The story has no tension. This writer's story is flat, without any sense of conflict or tension. The story is more of a chronicle than a story. If there is a problem, there is no build-up around possible solutions. Instead, the dog is simply lost and then found.	You told what happened in your story, in order, so I get it. But to make this into the kind of story that readers can't put down, the kind that readers read by flashlight in bed, you have to add what writers call edge-of-the-seat tension. Instead of just saying I did this, I did this, I did this, you need to have the narrator want something really badly and then run into difficulties, or trouble ... so readers are thinking, "Will it work? Won't it?" You've got to get readers all wound up! Right now, reread and find the part of the story where you could show what the main character really wants.	Edge-of-the-seat tension: 1. Someone really wants something. 2. Someone encounters trouble. 3. Someone tries, tries, tries.

If ...	After acknowledging what the child is doing well, you might say ...	Leave the writer with ...
The story has no real or significant ending. This writer has ended her story in a way that feels disappointing to the reader. Occasionally this will be because she has left loose ends unresolved, but most often it is because the ending of the story has little to do with the significance of the story itself. The ending may be something like, "Then I went home," or "The End!" She needs help identifying what her story is really about and then crafting an ending that ties directly to that meaning.	Sometimes it seems like your endings just trail off, and they aren't as powerful as they could be because of that. Writers know that the ending of a story is the last thing with which a reader will be left. Today, I want to teach you one tip for writing an ending that is particularly powerful. Writers ask, "What is this story really about?" Once they have the answer to that, they decide on a bit of dialogue or internal thinking, a descriptive detail, or a small action that will end the story in a way that ties back to that meaning.	Writers end a story in a way that shows what the story is **really** about. They might do this by including: • Dialogue • Internal thinking • A descriptive detail • A small action that ties back to the true meaning behind the story
The writer is new to the writing workshop or this particular genre of writing. This writer struggles because narrative is a new genre for her. She may display certain skill sets (e.g., the ability to use beautifully descriptive language or literary devices) but lacks the vision of what she is being asked to produce. Her story is probably long and unfocused and is usually dominated by summary, not storytelling.	Someone famously once said, "You can't hit a target if you don't know what that target is." This is especially true for writers. They can't write well if they don't have a vision, a mental picture, of what they hope to produce. Today, I want to teach you that one way writers learn about the kinds of writing they hope to produce is by studying mentor texts. They read a mentor text once, enjoying it as a story. Then, they read it again, this time asking, "How does this kind of story seem to go?" They label what they notice and then try it in their own writing.	Writers use mentor texts to help them imagine what they hope to write. They: • Read the text and enjoy it as a good story. • Reread the text and ask, "How does this kind of story seem to go?" • Note what they notice. • Try to do some of what they noticed in their own writing.
The writer does not use paragraphs. This writer does not use paragraphs to separate the different parts of his story. Because of this, the story is difficult to read and hold onto. He needs support understanding the importance of paragraphs, as well as the various ways writers use them.	Your writing will be a thousand times easier to read when you start using paragraphs. A paragraph is like a signal to a reader. It says, "Halt! Take a tiny break. Do you understand what is happening so far? Okay, I'm going to keep going!" Paragraphs give your readers an opportunity to take in your stories, and they also alert readers to important things like scene changes and new dialogue. Today, I want to teach you a few of the ways writers use paragraphs. Writers use paragraphs when a new event is starting, when their story is switching to a new time or place, when a new character speaks, or to separate out an important part that needs space around it.	Make a New Paragraph Here: • Very important part that needs space around it • New event • New time • New place • New character speaks
Elaboration		
The writer has created a story that is sparse, with little elaboration. This writer has written a story that is short, with one or more parts that need elaboration. He has conveyed the main outline of an event (this happened, then this happened, then this happened), but there is no sense that he has expanded on any one particular part.	You have gotten skilled at telling what happens, in order, but you write with just the bare bones sequence. Like, if you went out for supper yesterday and I asked you, "How was your dinner at the restaurant?" and you answered, "I went to the restaurant. I ate food. It was good." That's not the best story, right? It is just the bare bones with no flesh on them—like a skeleton. Can you try to flesh out your story?	Not: I ate food. I came home. But: Details, details, details.

If …	After acknowledging what the child is doing well, you might say …	Leave the writer with …
The story is riddled with details. In an attempt to elaborate or make a story compelling, the writer has listed what seem to be an endless number of tangential details. ("I got on the ride. There were a lot of people there. I was wearing a bright red shirt with a little giraffe on it. I was eating funnel cake.") This sort of elaboration often makes the piece feel monotonous, as if there is no real purpose guiding the writer's choice of details.	Although you are great at including details, you actually choose too many details. Writers are choosy about the details they include in a story. They know they can't include every detail they remember, so they have to decide which parts of their story to stretch out with details and which parts to move through more quickly. Writers ask, "What is this story really about?" and then stretch out the part of the story that goes with that meaning. Then, they cut details from the parts that are less important.	Although it is great to write with details—some writers write with too many details. Writers need to decide which details to **keep** and which to **cut**. They: • Ask, "What is my story really about?" • Stretch out the heart of the story. • Shorten less important parts.
The story is swamped with dialogue. This writer is attempting to story-tell, not summarize, but is relying too heavily on dialogue to accomplish this mission. The story is full of endless dialogue ("Let's play at the park," I said. "Okay," Jill said. "Maybe we should play on the swings," I said. "I agree," Jill said. "Great!" I said.). This writer needs to learn that dialogue is an important part of storytelling but cannot be the only device a writer uses to move a story forward.	Sometimes, writers make their characters talk—and talk and talk and talk. Today, I want to teach you that writers use dialogue, but they use it sparingly. They make sure their writing has a balance of action and dialogue by alternating between the two and by cutting dialogue that does not give the reader important information about the character or the story.	Writers make sure that their writing has a balance of dialogue and action: • They often alternate between action and dialogue as they write. • They cut dialogue that does not give the reader important information about the character or story.
The writer has written the external story but not the internal story. This writer has captured the events of a story precisely, and likely has done a fine job of moving the story along at an appropriate pace. What is missing, however, is the internal story. That is, as each event occurs, the main character is merely swept along with the current of events ("'Don't you ever do that again!' my dad yelled. He wagged his finger at me. I went up to my room and sat down to do my homework.") and has little emotional response. The reader is left wondering what the main character is feeling and thinking throughout the story, and as a result, the story lacks a certain depth.	When we first learn to write stories, we learn to tell the events that happened. We tell what happened first, then next, then next. As we become strong writers, though, it's important not just to write the external story, but also to write the internal story. Today, I want to teach you that when planning for and drafting a story, the writer plans not just the actions, but also the character's *reactions* to the events.	Writers tell not just what happened in a story—the **actions**—but also how the character felt about each of those events—the **reactions**.

If …	After acknowledging what the child is doing well, you might say …	Leave the writer with …
The writer struggles to identify and convey a deeper meaning. This writer's story likely contains most of the surface elements you are looking for but seems to lack a sense of purpose. When asked why she is writing this particular piece or what she hopes to convey to her reader, she struggles to find an answer. Because of this, each part of the story is often given equal attention, without any one part having been elaborated on. Dialogue, details, and other forms of narrative craft are used to move the story forward but do not contribute to the reader's understanding of the meaning or theme.	Everybody has stories to tell. At a certain point in your life as a writer, knowing *why* you want to tell these stories becomes almost as important as writing them. What I mean by this, and what I want to teach you today, is that writers reflect on the moments of their lives and ask, "What is this story really about? What do I want my reader to know about me?" Then, they use all they know about narrative craft to bring that meaning forward.	Writers ask: • What is this story really about? • What do I want my reader to know about me? Then they use all they know about narrative craft to bring that meaning forward.
The writer is ready to use literary devices. This writer is successfully using a variety of narrative techniques and would benefit from learning to use literary devices. He has a clear sense of the meaning behind his story, as well as the places where this meaning might be emphasized or further revealed.	I think you are ready for a new challenge. When writers are strong—using all sorts of craft, writing focused, well-paced stories—it often signals that they are ready for something new. I've noticed that you are trying to bring out what your story is really about, and I want to teach you one way that writers do this: using literary devices. Writers use comparisons (like metaphors and similes), repetition, and even symbols to highlight important messages in stories.	Literary devices writers use to reveal meaning to a reader: • Metaphors and similes • Repetition • Symbolism
The writer summarizes rather than story-tells. There is probably a sense that this writer is disconnected from the series of events—listing what happened first, then next, then next. He writes predominately by overviewing what happened ("On the way to school I was almost attacked by a dog but I got there okay."). The writer rarely uses dialogue, descriptive details, or other forms of narrative craft to convey the story to his reader.	Writers don't take huge steps through their experience, writing like this: "I had an argument. Then I went to bed." Instead, writers take tiny steps, writing more like this: "'It was your turn!' I yelled, and then I turned and walked out of the room really fast. I slammed the door and went to my bedroom. I was so furious that I just sat on my bed for a long time." It helps to show what happened rather than just telling the main gist of it.	Not giant steps, but baby steps. Show, not tell.

If ...	After acknowledging what the child is doing well, you might say ...	Leave the writer with ...
Language		
The writer struggles with spelling. This writer's piece is riddled with spelling mistakes. This does not necessarily mean the writing is not strong (in fact, the story may be very strong), but the spelling mistakes compromise the reader's ability to understand it. The writer's struggle with spelling may stem from various places—difficulty understanding and applying spelling patterns, a limited stock of high-frequency words, lack of investment, the acquisition of English as a new language—and diagnosing the underlying problem will be an important precursor to teaching into it.	One of the things I'm noticing about your writing is how beautiful it sounds when you read it aloud. I looked more closely, curious about how I had missed all the beauty you've captured on this page, and realized that all your spelling mistakes make it difficult for me (and probably other readers, too) to understand. Today, I want to teach you a few techniques writers use to help them spell. Writers use the classroom word wall, they stretch words out and write down the sounds they hear, and they use words they *do* know how to spell to help them with those they don't know how to spell.	Writers work hard at their spelling. They: • Use the **word wall**. • **S-T-R-E-T-C-H** words out and write down the sounds they hear. • Use words they **know** (*found*), to help them spell words they **don't know** (*compound*, *round*).
The writer struggles with end punctuation. This story amounts to what appears to be one long, endless sentence. The writer may have distinct sentences ("We ran down the road James was chasing us we thought we needed to run faster to escape him") that are simply not punctuated. Alternatively, he may have strung his sentences together using an endless number of *and*s, *then*s, and *but*s in an attempt at cohesion. ("We ran down the road and James was chasing us and we thought that we needed to run faster to escape him but then we could hear his footsteps and his breathing and we were scared.")	I read your piece today, and it sounded a bit like this. "We ran down the road and James was chasing us and we thought that we needed to run faster to escape him but then we could hear his footsteps and his breathing and we were scared." Phew, I was out of breath! Today, I want to teach you that writers use end punctuation to give their readers a little break, to let them take a breath, before moving on to the next thing that happened in the story. One way to figure out where to put end punctuation is to reread your piece aloud, notice where you find yourself stopping to take a small breath, and put a period, exclamation point, or question mark there.	Writers reread their pieces aloud, notice where readers should stop and take a small breath because one thought has ended, and use end punctuation to help mark those places.
The Process of Generating Ideas		
The writer has "nothing to write about." This writer often leaves the minilesson, returns to his seat, and sits idly, waiting for you to visit. When you do visit, he is generally quick to tell you that he has "nothing to write about." This writer needs help with independence, but also with understanding that life is one big source of stories. As long as one is living, one has something to write about!	I'm noticing that you often have trouble finding things to write about, and I wanted to remind you that life is one big source of story ideas. Writers see the world through special eyes, imagining stories in the tiniest of moments. Writers find stories at the dinner table, while walking down the street, in the classroom, and at recess. Writers know that it matters less *what* they write about and more *how* they write about it.	Writers have the eyes to find stories everywhere. They know it matters less **what** they write about and more **how** they write about it.

If …	After acknowledging what the child is doing well, you might say …	Leave the writer with …
The writer's notebook work does not represent all she can do. This writer is content to summarize and write in cursory ways in her notebook, and does not hold herself to using all she knows when collecting entries. This may mean the entries are short, underdeveloped, or lack narrative craft. When you look at this child's entries, you do not get the sense that she is striving to do her best work while collecting.	Many people think that the writer's notebook is just a place to collect stuff and that real writing happens when you pick a seed idea and draft on lined paper. I sort of get the idea you think that way. It is true that the notebook is a place for collecting, but it is also true that the notebook is a place for *practicing*. Today, I want to teach you that writers hold themselves accountable for using everything they know about good writing whenever they write, even in their notebooks. This includes everything they know about structure, storytelling, revision, and editing!	Writers use their notebooks to practice becoming better writers. They use everything they know about structure, storytelling, and even revision and editing!
The Process of Drafting		
The writer has trouble maintaining stamina and volume. This writer has a hard time putting words down on the page. It may be that he writes for a long period of time producing very little or that he refuses to write for longer than a few minutes. The writer often has avoidance behaviors (e.g., trips to the bathroom during writing workshop, a pencil tip that breaks repeatedly). He gets very little writing done during the workshop, despite urging from you.	Today, I want to teach you a little trick that often works for me when I'm having trouble staying focused. When writing is hard for me, I set small, manageable goals for myself. I make sure these goals are something I *know* I can do, like writing for ten minutes straight. Then, when I reach my goal, I give myself a little gift, like a short walk or a few minutes to sketch a picture. Then, I get back to writing again.	Writers set goals for themselves and work hard to achieve them. When they do, they reward themselves for their hard work.
The writer struggles to work independently. This student is often at your side, asking questions or needing advice. She struggles to write on her own and only seems to generate ideas when you are sitting beside her. When she does write, she needs constant "checks" and accolades. She is task-oriented. That is, she will complete one thing you have taught her to do and then sit and wait to be told what to do next. She does not rely on charts or other materials to keep her going.	As a writer, it is important that you take control of your own writing life. You can't be content to sit back and relax. Instead, you have to ask yourself, "What in this room might help me get back on track as a writer?" Then, you use those resources to get started again. You can look at charts in the room, ask your partner for help, read mentor texts for inspiration, or even look back over old writing for new ideas. OR One thing I'm noticing about you as a writer is that you write with me in mind. What I mean by this is that when I teach something, you try it. When I suggest something, you try it. But I am not the only writing teacher in this room. Believe it or not, *you* can be your own writing teacher, too. Today, I want to teach you how to look at your own work against a checklist, assess for what is going well and what you might do better, and then set goals for how you might revise your current piece and for what you might try out in your future work, too.	When you are stuck, you can: • Consult charts • Ask your partner for help • Read mentor texts for inspiration • Look back over old writing for new ideas

If...	After acknowledging what the child is doing well, you might say ...	Leave the writer with ...
The Process of Revision		
The writer does not seem to be driven by personal goals as much as by your instruction. If you ask, "What are you working on?" this writer acts surprised. "My writing," she says, and indeed, you are pretty sure that is what she is doing. She is trying to crank out the required amount of text. She doesn't have more specific goals about how to do things better that are influencing her.	Can I ask you something? Who is the boss of your writing? I'm asking that because you need to be the boss of your writing, and to be the best boss you can be, you need to give yourself little assignments. You need to take yourself by the hand and say, "From now on, you should be working on this," and then after a bit, "Now you should be working on this."	My Writing Goals Are: 1. _____ 2. _____ 3. _____
The Process of Editing		
The writer does not use what she knows about editing while writing. This writer is not applying what she knows about spelling, grammar, and punctuation while writing. You may notice that you have taught a particular spelling pattern, and she mastered it in isolation but is not using that knowledge during writing workshop. She may also spell word wall words incorrectly or misspell words that are similar (e.g., spelling *getting* correctly but misspelling *setting*). This writer needs to be reminded that editing is not something left for the last stages of writing. Instead, writers use all they know *as they write*.	You are the boss of your own writing, and part of being the boss is making sure that you are doing, and using, everything you know while you write. Often when people think of editing, they think of it as something they do just before publishing. This is true, but it is also true that writers edit as they write. Today, I want to teach you that writers use an editing checklist to remind them of what they've learned about spelling, punctuation, and grammar. They take a bit of time each day to make sure they are using all they know as they write.	Editing Checklist • Read, asking, "Will this make sense to a stranger?" • Check the punctuation. • Do your words look like they are spelled correctly?

Information Writing

If ...	After acknowledging what the child is doing well, you might say ...	Leave the writer with ...
Structure and Cohesion		
The writer has not established a clear organizational structure. This writer is struggling with organization. It is likely that his book is a jumble of information about a larger topic, with no clear subheadings or internal organization. The writer may have a table of contents but the chapters actually contain a whole bunch of stuff unrelated to the chapter titles, or the writer may have skipped this part of the process altogether.	One of the most important things information writers do is organize their writing. Making chapters or headings is one way to make it easier for your readers to learn about your topic. It's like creating little signs that say, "Hey, reader, I'm about to start talking about a new part of my topic!" It helps to name what the upcoming part of your writing will be about and then to write about just that thing. When information writers notice they are about to start writing about something new, they often create a new heading that tells the reader what the next part will be about.	One thing _____ About that thing About that thing About that thing Another thing _____ About that next thing About that next thing ~~Something else~~ ~~Something else~~ Another thing _____ NOT: One thing Another thing The first thing A whole other thing
There is no logical order to the sequence of information. The writer has a clearly structured piece of writing and is ready to consider the logical order of the different sections of information. That is, she is ready to think about what sections of her text will come first, which will fall in the middle, and which will come last. In doing so, she will consider audience, as well as the strength of each part of her writing.	You are ready for a big new step. After writers learn to organize an information piece and have created perfectly structured sections and parts, they are often left asking, "What's next?" *What's next* is organizing again but doing it with more purpose. What I mean is this: writers ask, "Which part of my text should come first? Which should come second? What about third?" They think about what order makes the most sense for their particular topic. They might decide to organize from least to most important information, from weakest to strongest information, in chronological order, or in other ways.	Information writers sort their information **logically**. They might put the sections in order from least to most important, weakest to strongest, chronologically, or in other ways.

If ...	After acknowledging what the child is doing well, you might say ...	Leave the writer with ...
Information in various sections overlaps. This writer attempted to organize his piece, but has various sections that overlap. The writer may have repeated similar information in several parts of his piece or may have attempted to give the same information worded differently. Often he has sections and subsections that are too closely related and therefore struggles to find different information for different parts.	It is great that you have a system for organizing things. It is sort of like this page is a drawer and you just put things about (XYZ) in it. And this chapter is a drawer and you just put stuff about (ABC) in it. There are a few mess-ups—places where you have some whole other things scattered in, or some things that are in two places. That always happens. You've got to expect it. So what writers do is just what you have done. They write organized pieces. But then, when they are done writing, they ... Do you know? They reread to check. Just like you can reread to check your spelling, you can reread to check that the right things are in the right drawers, the right sections.	Writers reread to check that things are in the right drawers.
The writer is ready to experiment with alternative organizational structures. This writer may have a relatively strong organizational structure to her information piece, but you sense there are better options or more challenging avenues she might take. Then too, she may have tried to organize her piece one way, but the topic does not lend itself well to the structure she has chosen. In either instance, she is ready to broaden her repertoire in regard to organizational structure and study mentor texts to imagine alternate ways her text might go.	One of the greatest things about information writing is that there are so many different ways a text can go. If we were to lay out a few different books on the same topic, we would find dozens of different ways the authors chose to organize them. Some authors, like Gail Gibbons, write chronologically, others write about different sections of a topic, and some authors use pros and cons or questions and answers to organize their information. The options are endless! When writers are looking to challenge themselves and try out some new ways of organizing their writing, they study mentor texts. One way to study an information text is to read, asking, "How does this author structure and organize his information?" Then, you can try out the same structure with your own writing.	Information writers study mentor texts and ask, "How does this author structure and organize his information? Then, they try the same with their own writing.
The writer has chosen a topic that is too broad. This writer has chosen a topic that is broad, such as dogs or the Civil War, and has likely created a table of contents that suggests the product will be more of an all-about book. In an attempt to make his writing more sophisticated, and the process of crafting an information piece more demanding, you will want to teach him to narrow his topic a bit.	I was looking at your topic choice earlier and thought to myself, "He is ready for a challenge!" You chose a topic that is very broad, very big. There is nothing wrong with that. In fact, it means you'll have a lot to say! But when information writers want to push themselves, when they want to craft a text that is more sophisticated, they narrow their topic. Today, I'm going to teach you how to narrow your topic by asking, "What is *one part* of this subject I can write a lot about?"	Writers challenge themselves by narrowing their topics. They ask, "What is *one part* of this subject I can write a lot about?"

If …	After acknowledging what the child is doing well, you might say …	Leave the writer with …
The piece lacks an introduction and/or a conclusion. This writer has written an information piece that is missing an introduction and/or conclusion. Alternatively, it may be that the writer attempted to introduce and then conclude her piece but did so in overly folksy or ineffective ways. (For instance, she might have begun, "My name is Michelle, and I'm going to teach you everything you want to know about sharks. They are really cool." Later, she'll likely end along the same lines: "That's everything about sharks! I hope you learned a lot!") She is ready to adopt a more sophisticated tone and learn more nuanced (and subtle) ways of pulling readers in and providing closure.	In stories, writers use introductions to pull their readers in. Their conclusions, or endings, usually give the reader some closure. Really, information writing isn't much different. Writers use introductions to *pull* readers in, often by giving them a little information on the topic (orienting them). Then, they give their reader a sense of closure by wrapping things up with a conclusion (sometimes restating some key points about the topic) and leaving the reader with something to think about.	Introductions pull readers in: • Give a bit of information about the topic. Orient your reader. Conclusions give readers closure and wrap things up: • Restate a bit about the topic. • Leave your reader with something to think about.
Elaboration		
Each section is short and needs elaboration. This writer has attempted to group her information, but each section is short. For example, she may have listed one or two facts related to a specific subsection but is stuck for what to add next.	Information writers need to be able to say a lot about each part of their topic, or to elaborate. There are a few things you can do to make each part of your book chock-full of information. One thing that helps is to write in partner sentences. This means that instead of writing one sentence about each thing, you can push yourself to write two sentences (or more) about each thing. So if I said, "George sits at a desk when he is at school" and I wanted to write with partner sentences, what else might I say about George sitting at his desk?" You are right. It can help to fill in stuff about why, kinds of, where, how many, and so on. A whole other thing you can do to get yourself to say more is to use prompts like, "It's also important to know this because …"; "Also …"; and "What this means is …"	Writers Elaborate 1. They check to make sure they have at least four or five pieces of information for each subtopic. If not, they consider cutting that section and starting a new one. 2. Writers elaborate by creating partner sentences. 3. They use prompts like "It's also important to know …"; "Also …"; and "What this means is …" to say more about a particular piece of information.

If ...	After acknowledging what the child is doing well, you might say ...	Leave the writer with ...
The writer elaborates by adding fact upon fact. This writer has elaborated but has done so by adding fact upon fact upon fact. As a result, his writing reads like a list rather than a cohesive section of text. This writer would benefit from learning to add a bit of his own voice back into his writing, relying not just on factual information, but on his own ability to synthesize and make sense of these facts for the reader.	You have tackled the first step in information writing—gathering the information needed to support various subtopics. Here's the thing, though. Writers don't *just* list facts for readers. It is also their job to take these facts and make something of them, to help explain why they are important to the reader. Writers often use prompts like "In other words ... ," "What this really means is ... ," "This shows ... ," and "All of this is important because ..." to help readers understand the information they've put forth.	Information writers don't just list fact after fact. They *spice up* their writing by adding a bit of their own voice: • "In other words ..." • "What this really means is ..." • "This shows ..." • "All of this is important because ..."
The writer goes off on tangents when elaborating. This writer has tried to elaborate on information but tends to get into personal and tangential details ("Dogs really are great pets. I have a dog, too. I had a cat, too, but she peed on the counter so my Dad got rid of her.") Or by repeating the same information again and again. Or by being chit-chatty ("And I love LOVE that and think it is really funny, so so funny.").	You are working hard to say a lot about your topic, aren't you? I have to give you a tip, though. Sometimes, in your hard work to say a lot, you are doing things that don't really work that well. Let me give you an example of things that don't work when writers are writing information books, and will you see if you do those things some of the time? Pretend I was writing about dogs, so I wrote that there are many kinds of dogs, and the kinds of dogs are divided into groups, like spaniels, retrievers, toy dogs, and so forth. If I then said, "And I have a dog and a cat, too, and the cat's name is Barney ..." would that go in my report? You are right. It wouldn't go because it isn't really teaching information and ideas about the topic—and it might not even be about the topic. If I wrote "And I Love Love LOVE dogs," would that go? And if I said, "Some dogs are spaniels, some are retrievers," would that go? You see, there are things people do when they are trying to elaborate, to say more, that just don't work that well. So what writers do is they cross them out and try other ways to elaborate. You will want to reread your writing and to have the courage to say no sometimes. OR Today, I want to teach you that information writers revise by checking to make sure all their information is important and new. They cut out parts where they started to talk about their own life too much and got off topic, parts where they included information that doesn't go with what they were writing about, or parts where they repeat the same thing.	Information writers cut parts where: • They started talking about their life too much and got off topic. • They included information that doesn't fit with what the rest of the paragraph is about. • They repeated something they'd already written.

If ...	After acknowledging what the child is doing well, you might say ...	Leave the writer with ...
The writer does not elaborate on information from outside sources. The writer has included information from outside sources, such as quotes, facts, or statistics, but does not elaborate on this information for his reader. As a result, his writing is often very short and hops from interesting fact to interesting fact.	I love all the research you have included in your information piece. It really shows that you are an expert on this topic. One way to show you are an expert, to show all you know about your topic, is by including outside information like quotes, facts, and statistics. Another way to be an expert and teach your readers (the way I'm going to teach you today) is by elaborating on those facts. Today, I want to teach you that writers don't just plop information into their writing. Instead, they explain what it means to their readers by using phrases like "What this means is ..." or "In other words ..."	Writers don't just plop information into their writing. Instead, they explain what it means to their readers by using phrases like "What this means is ..." or "In other words ..."
Language		
The writer incorporates quotes, facts, and statistics but does so awkwardly. This writer uses quotes, facts, statistics, and other outside information to elaborate on the sections of his information text. The information is well organized, and the facts and quotes are generally well placed but often sound awkward. It is not clear that the writer understands how to move from his words to the words and examples of an author or experts, and he needs help with ways to do this more fluently.	Quotes, facts, and statistics are incredibly important in information writing because they tell a reader that, yes, I have done my research and know a lot about my topic! Today, I want to teach you how to take quotes, facts, and statistics and make them sound like a part of your writing. You can do this by using transitional phrases like *for instance*, *one example*, or *according to*.	Writers use transitional phrases to introduce quotes, facts, and statistics. <u>Example:</u> Sharks aren't that dangerous. One example of this is basking sharks. People in the Hamptons often see them and they are slow-moving and harmless. According to Science-Facts.com, "more people die of alligator attacks than shark attacks."
Transitions from section to section sound awkward. This writer has organized her information piece into sections and paragraphs, but the transitions from part to part feel awkward. She would benefit from a few tips aimed at helping her ease readers into each new section of her text.	One of the hardest parts about being an information writer is moving from one part of a topic to the next. One second a writer is talking about the Lewis and Clark expedition, and the next second she is talking about the Louisiana Purchase. In her mind she knows how these two things connect (they are both about the Westward Expansion), but this isn't always clear to her readers. Today, I want to teach you how to write a topic sentence that reminds readers what your big topic is and introduces them to what your next section will be about. One way writers do this is by connecting each section back to the larger topic.	Information writers use topic sentences to say what a section will be about and explain how it relates to the big, overall topic. <u>Example:</u> Lewis and Clark were famous explorers who took on a daring adventure. They were an important part of the Westward Expansion. or Another important part of the Westward Expansion was the Louisiana Purchase, because it gave Americans new land to explore and settle.

If …	After acknowledging what the child is doing well, you might say …	Leave the writer with …
The writer does not incorporate domain-specific vocabulary. This writer has written about a topic but has done so without incorporating domain-specific vocabulary. It may be that the child simply glossed over using terms such as *caravan* or *brigade* (because he did not understand them or know how to incorporate them into his own writing) or used simpler language in place of complex vocabulary.	As an information writer, it's important that you come across as an expert on your topic. Readers expect to learn something new, and one way to teach them something new is by using technical, expert vocabulary. Today, I want to teach you that writers don't just toss these words into their writing, though. Instead, they learn what they mean, and then they define them for their readers. They can either say the word and then its definition, or tuck the word's definition into a sentence using commas.	Information writers use expert vocabulary (and define it for their readers, too). They can: • Say the word and then explain what it means. Example: Loyalists were people who remained loyal to the king during the American Revolution. • Tuck the definition into the sentence using two commas. Example: Loyalists, people who remained loyal to the king during the American Revolution, fought throughout the war.
The Process of Generating Ideas		
The writer chooses topics about which she has little expertise and/or that are difficult to research. This child often generates ideas quickly, and they often relate to her passions. She might decide to write about the melting of the polar ice caps and its effect on seals during a unit in which students are writing about areas of personal expertise or access to research material on that topic is limited and difficult to comprehend. This child needs help mining her life for topics that are closer to home and assessing her own ability to write long, strong, and focused about a particular topic.	Writers ask themselves some tough questions when they are choosing a topic for information writing. They ask: 1. Do I care about this topic? (You are already doing this!) 2. Do I know enough to imagine a possible table of contents? 3. Do I know one or two resources I can use to gather more information? If not, they pick a different topic.	When Choosing a Topic, Information Writers Ask: • Do I care about this topic? • Do I know enough to imagine a possible table of contents? • Do I know one or two resources I can use to gather more information?
The writer simply copies facts into his notebook. This writer's "collecting" amounts to copying facts from books into his notebook. He copies lines verbatim, rarely bothering to paraphrase or quote. It may seem as if the child is not being overly discriminatory about what to include. That is, if the book says it, he writes it. In this way, the child's notebook becomes an endless list of facts about a topic or, if the child has created organized categories, parts of a topic.	Research is a pretty hard thing to do as a writer. Researchers have a difficult job: They have to take the information that other people have written, sort through it, and then put it into their own words or quote it. You can't just copy what other authors have written into your notebook, because that would be stealing their words! Today, I want to teach you one way that writers take information from a book and incorporate it into their own writing. It's called *paraphrasing*. To paraphrase (or put something into your own words), it helps to read a chunk of text, close the book, say back an important part of what you just read, and then put it into your own words.	One way researchers put information into their own words is by paraphrasing. They: 1. Read a chunk of the text. 2. Close the book. 3. Say back an important part of what they just read. 4. Put it into their own words.

If ...	After acknowledging what the child is doing well, you might say ...	Leave the writer with ...
The Process of Drafting		
The first draft is not organized. This writer has written a first draft that is disorganized. It may be that there is an underlying organizational structure (e.g., the writer grouped similar information together), but she did not use new pages, section titles, or transitions to let the reader in on this structure. Alternatively, the writer may have simply "written a draft," compiling all the information she collected into one ongoing piece of writing.	One of the most important things information writers do is organize. It can be hard for a reader to learn a lot of new information about, say, sharks. But when a writer organizes the information into sections, then it becomes easier for the reader to take it in. The reader knows that one part will be about sharks' bodies, another will be about what they eat, and another will be about their family life. As a writer, it's important to look at your draft and make sure that you've organized it in a way that will make sense to the reader. This usually means taking all the information or facts about one part of a topic (like sharks' bodies) and putting that together. Then, taking all the information about another topic (like what sharks eat) and putting that together. Then using section headings to make it clear what each part is about.	Information Writers Organize Their Writing! • Divide your topic into sections (you may have already done this while planning). • Put the information about one section together with a heading. • Put the information about another section together with a heading. • And so on ... (Sometimes it helps to cut up your draft and tape different parts together!)
The Process of Revision		
The writer is "done" before revising. This writer is perfectly pleased with his first draft and declares, "I'm done" soon after completing it. Your revision minilessons do little to help inspire this writer to revise, and you feel you must constantly sit by his side and point out parts to revise in order for him to do the work.	I've noticed that you often have trouble thinking of ways to revise your piece. You write a draft and then it feels done. Sometimes when it is hard to come up with ideas for improving your writing, it helps to have a published writer help. You just look at a published book that you love and notice cool things that the author has done, then you revise to do those same things in your writing.	When writers feel done, they study a few mentor texts asking, "What has this writer done that I could try as well?"
The writer does not have a large repertoire of strategies to draw from. This writer lives off of each day's minilesson. She is task-oriented and generally applies (or attempts to apply) what you teach each day. This student is living on your day-to-day teaching as if it is all she has, rather than drawing on a large repertoire of known writing techniques and strategies.	Whenever I teach something, I love to see kids like you go off and give it a go. It means they are pushing themselves to try new things. But I also hope that isn't *all* kids do. We've talked about how writers carry invisible backpacks full of strategies. When I teach a minilesson, I give you something new to add to your backpack, but it is important to use everything else you have in there, too! Today, I want to teach you one way writers remind themselves of what they already know about revision. They look at artifacts like classroom charts and our information writing checklist and look back at old entries to remind themselves of the strategies they know. Then, they write an action plan.	Take Action! 1. Look at charts, your notebook, and the Information Writing Checklist. 2. Make a list of the ways you could revise. 3. Create an action plan for yourself.

If ...	After acknowledging what the child is doing well, you might say ...	Leave the writer with ...
The Process of Editing		
The writer has edited but has missed several mistakes or would otherwise benefit from learning to partner-edit. This writer often thinks she has written what she intended to say, and therefore she overlooks many mistakes. She would benefit from learning to edit with a partner before publishing her writing.	I know that you have worked hard to use many of the editing strategies you know and have made many changes to your piece. As a result, it is clearer and more readable. Sometimes as a writer, though, you know so clearly what you *wanted* to say that you miss places where you may have said something in a confusing or incorrect way. That's why most writers have editors that look at their writing once it's done. Today, I want to teach you a few things you and your writing partner can do together. You can: • Read your piece aloud and ask your partner to check to make sure what you say matches what he or she sees. • Circle words you think are misspelled and try to figure them out together. • Use the class editing checklist together.	A Few Things You and Your Writing Partner Might Say to Each Other • "Reread your piece, and I'll make sure what you say matches what I see." • "Let's circle the words that we think are misspelled and try them again." • "Let's use our class editing checklist to proofread your piece."

Opinion Writing

If …	After acknowledging what the child is doing well, you might say …	Leave the writer with …
Structure and Cohesion		

The introduction does not forecast the structure of the essay.
 	
The writer has made a claim and supported it with reasons, but there is no forecasting statement early on in the essay that foreshadows the reasons to come. Instead, it seems as if the writer thought of and wrote about one reason, then, when reaching the end of that first body paragraph, thought, "What's another reason?" and then raised and elaborated upon that reason. He is ready to learn to plan for the overarching structure of his argument and forecast that structure in the introduction.
	You have definitely learned to make a claim in your essay and to support that claim with reasons. There is one big step you need to take, though, and that is to let your reader know how your essay will go from the very beginning, in the introduction. Today, I want to teach you that opinion writers forecast how their writing will go. They do this by stating their claim in the introduction and then adding on, "I think this because …" Then they list the reasons that they will write about in the body of their piece.	Writers use the introduction to forecast how their opinion pieces will go.
		
		1. State your claim.
		   • "I think …"
		2. Tell your reader why your claim is true.
		   • "One reason I think … is because …"
		   • "Another reason I think … is because …"
		   • "The final reason I think … is because …"

Supports overlap. In this instance, the writer has developed supporting reasons that are overlapping or overly similar. While this may pose few problems now, the writer will struggle when the time comes to find examples to support each reason (because the examples will be the same!). For example, if a student argues, "Dogs make the best pets," she may provide the following reasons: they like to play games, they cheer you up, and they are great at playing fetch. Playing fetch and playing games overlap, and you'll want to help this student find another, different, reason why dogs are great pets.	Sometimes, when writers develop supporting reasons for their thesis, they find that one or more of them overlap. What I mean by this is that they basically say the same thing! Today, I want to teach you that writers look at their supporting reasons with a critical eye, checking to see if any overlap. One way they do this is by listing the examples they'll use for each paragraph. If some of the examples are the same, then the reasons are probably too similar!	Are your supporting reasons too similar? Test them to find out! Support _____ Example #1: Example #2: Support _____ Example #1: Example #2: Support _____ Example #1: Example #2:

If …	After acknowledging what the child is doing well, you might say …	Leave the writer with …
Supports are not parallel or equal in weight. This writer has developed a thesis and supports. While all the supports may support the writer's overall claim, they are not parallel. For instance, when arguing that "dogs make great friends," the writer may have suggested that this is because (A) they always listen to you, (B) they play with you, and (C) one time I was sad and my dog cuddled with me. Supports A and B are both reasons or ways that dogs can make great friends. Support C is an example of *one time* a dog made a good friend. This writer needs help identifying places where one or more supports are not parallel and/or are not equal in weight to the others.	As a writer, you want each part of your essay to be about equal in weight. What I mean by this is that all your supports should prove your overall claim *and* they should be something you can elaborate on with several examples. Today, I want to teach you that writers look back over their supports and ask, "Are these all equal in size?" One way they test out this question is by checking to see if they can give two to three examples for each support. If they can't, they have to revise the supporting reason to make it bigger.	Do you have examples to prove each of your supports? Support _____ Example #1: Example #2: Support _____ Example #1: Example #2: Support _____ Example #1: Example #2:
The writer is new to the writing workshop or this particular genre of writing. This writer struggles not because she has struggled to raise the level of her opinion writing, but because this is a new genre for her. She may display certain skill sets (e.g., the ability to elaborate or write with beautiful descriptions) but lacks the vision of what she is being asked to produce. Her piece may be unfocused or disorganized. It also may be sparse, lacking any sort of elaboration.	As a writer, it can be particularly hard to write well if you don't have a vision, a mental picture, of what you hope to produce. Today, I want to teach you that one way writers learn about the kinds of writing they hope to produce is by studying mentor texts. They read a mentor text once, enjoying it as a piece of writing. Then, they read it again, this time asking, "How do opinion pieces seem to go?" They label what they notice and then try it in their own writing.	Writers use mentor texts to help them imagine what they hope to write. They: 1. Read the text and enjoy it as a piece of writing. 2. Ask, "How do opinion pieces seem to go?" 3. Label what they notice. 4. Try some of what they noticed in their own writing.
The writer has a number of well-developed reasons, but they blur together without paragraphs or transitions. This writer has developed multiple reasons to support his opinion and has supported those reasons with evidence. It is difficult to discern an organizational structure in the piece, however, because many of the reasons blur together without paragraphs or transitions.	A paragraph is like a signal to a reader. It says, "I just made an important point. Now I'm moving on to something else." Paragraphs give readers an opportunity to take in evidence part by part, reason by reason. Readers expect that opinion writers will separate their reasons in paragraphs, with one section for each reason. Writers reread their writing, take note of when they've moved from one reason to another, and insert a paragraph there.	Opinion writers use paragraphs to separate their reasons. Each paragraph has: Reasons + Evidence

If ...	After acknowledging what the child is doing well, you might say ...	Leave the writer with ...
The writer is ready to consider counterarguments. This writer has shown evidence that she is ready to consider counterarguments. She may have written something like, "I know that not everyone agrees, but ..." or may have gone further and laid out the opposing argument that others might make. She is ready to learn to use counterarguments to bolster her own argument.	You are doing one of the hardest things there is to do when you are working to write an argument. You are imagining the people who might disagree with you and trying to see an opposite point of view from your own. Today, I want to show you how to raise the level of that work by teaching you to use counterarguments to *make your own argument stronger*! One way to do this is by showing that there are flaws or gaps or problems in the counterargument, and then show how *your* argument addresses those problems. So you might start by saying, "This argument overlooks ..." or "This argument isn't showing the full story."	Strong opinion writers expose the flaws, gaps, and problems in counterarguments and then show how their argument addresses those problems. They might begin: • "This argument overlooks ..." • "This argument isn't showing the full story."
Elaboration		
The writer is struggling to elaborate (1). This writer has an opinion, as well as several reasons to support that opinion, but most reasons are stated without elaboration. He may have created a long list of reasons to support his opinion, but does not say more about any one reason or provide examples or evidence to support his reasons.	You know that when you give an opinion, you need to support it with reasons! But opinion writers don't just stop with reasons. Today, I want to teach you that when writers come up with a reason to support a claim, they then try to write a whole paragraph about that reason. One way to do this is by shifting into a mini-story. You can start your claim and reason and then write, "For example, one day ..." or "For example, in the text ..." and tell a mini-story that shows and proves your reason.	One way writers elaborate on a reason is by providing a mini-story to prove their point. They might write: • "For example, one day ..." (personal essay) or • "For example, in the text ..." (literary or argument essay)
The writer is struggling to elaborate (2). This writer has an opinion, as well as several reasons to support that opinion, but most reasons are stated without elaboration. She may have created an endless list of reasons to support her opinion, but does not say more about any one reason or provide examples and evidence to support it. She has learned to use mini-stories to support her reasons and is ready for a larger repertoire of evidence.	You know that when you give an opinion, you need to support it with reasons! But opinion writers don't just stop with reasons. They need evidence to convince their readers that their claim is right. Today, I want to teach you that when writers come up with reasons to support a claim, they then try to write a whole paragraph about that reason. One way to do this is by adding facts, statistics, definitions, and quotes that support your reason. Writers have to choose the evidence that makes the most sense for them.	Opinion writers support reasons using: • Mini-stories • Facts • Statistics • Definitions • Quotes
The writer's evidence feels free-floating or disconnected from the argument at hand. This writer has elaborated on reasons using evidence but has done little to explain that evidence to his reader. He'll often drop a fact or statistic into a paragraph and may even recognize that it feels awkward. He needs strategies for elaborating on evidence, specifically by learning to tie it back to the overarching claim.	You have elaborated by providing not only reasons to support your claim, but evidence as well. Sometimes, when writers write persuasively, they incorporate facts and statistics and mini-stories, only to find that these feel awkward or disconnected from their own writing. Writers have a trick to fix this problem, and that is what I want to teach you today! One way writers make evidence particularly persuasive is by saying a bit about how that evidence relates to their claim. They might say, "This proves ..." or "This shows that _____ is true because ..."	Writers don't just toss evidence into an opinion piece. Instead, they help their readers understand why it is there! They can help explain the importance of the evidence by writing things like: • "This proves ..." • "This shows that ____ is true because ..."

If ...	After acknowledging what the child is doing well, you might say ...	Leave the writer with ...
The piece is swamped with details. This writer is attempting to be convincing and knows that details matter. His writing is riddled with facts, details, quotes, and other forms of evidence in support of his thesis. Because the writing is so detail-heavy, the writer has likely struggled to fully integrate the evidence or explain it to his reader.	You are the kind of writer who knows that details matter. Today, I want to teach you that choosing the just-right details and cutting others can make your piece even better. One way to know what details to keep and what details to cut is to read each piece of evidence and ask, "Is that evidence the *most* convincing evidence I can give to convince my readers of my opinion?" Then you make some hard choices—keeping the best evidence and cutting the rest.	Opinion writers choose evidence carefully and critically! • Look at each piece of evidence and ask, "Is that evidence the *most* convincing evidence I can give?" • Then, keep the best evidence and cut the rest.
The writer has provided evidence, but it does not all support the claim. This writer has elaborated on her reasons with a variety of evidence, but not all of this evidence matches the point she is trying to make. It may be that a mini-story is unfocused and not angled to support a particular point. It may be that a quote or statistic does not connect directly to the claim. Either way, this writer needs help rereading her piece with a critical lens, checking to be sure that each sentence she has written helps to further her opinion.	As a writer, you know it is important not just to give a bunch of reasons for a claim, but also to spend time *proving* those reasons. You have already done this by including all sorts of evidence. Today, I want to teach you that after collecting evidence, writers go back to look at their writing with a critical lens. They ask, "Does this piece of evidence match my reason? Does it really prove what I am trying to say?" If it matches, they keep it. If not, they cut it out.	Opinion writers ask: • Does this piece of evidence match my reason? • Does this prove what I am trying to say? If so, they keep it! If not, they cut it!
Language		
The writer uses a casual, informal tone when writing. As you read this writer's opinion pieces, you are overwhelmed by a sense of casualness and informality. Likely this comes from a good place on the writer's part. He may be trying to communicate directly with his audience. ("Hey, wait, stop and think before you throw that piece of garbage on the ground.") He may also be attempting to be convincing. ("Littering is SOOOO bad for the environment and kills animals every day!!") There is nothing wrong with this, but you sense that this writer is ready to move toward more sophisticated forms of persuasion, beginning with the adoption of a more formal, academic tone.	As an opinion writer, your first and foremost job is to convince readers that your claim, your opinion, is correct. When you first start out as a persuasive writer, you learn fun little ways to do this, like talking to the reader or making exaggerations. But as you grow as a writer, the challenge becomes, "How do I make my writing equally as persuasive but do it in a way that sounds more sophisticated, more professional, more grown up?" Today, I want to teach you a few tricks for adopting a more formal tone in your writing. When writers want to sound more formal they: • Use expert vocabulary • Use sophisticated transition words and phrases • Incorporate startling facts from credible sources	Sound like an expert! • Use expert vocabulary related to your topic. Example: When talking about the environment you might use words like, *biodegradable* or *ozone* • Use sophisticated transition words to introduce insights, ideas, or examples. Examples: *alternately, additionally, furthermore* • Incorporate startling facts from credible sources. Example: "You may not have known that, according to recycling-revolution.com, recycling one aluminum can saves enough energy to power a TV for three hours!

If …	After acknowledging what the child is doing well, you might say …	Leave the writer with …
The writer struggles with spelling. This writer's piece is riddled with spelling mistakes. This does not necessarily mean the writing is not strong (in fact, the essay he wrote may be very strong), but the spelling mistakes compromise the reader's ability to understand it. The writer's struggle with spelling may stem from various causes—difficulty with understanding and applying spelling patterns, a limited stock of high-frequency words, lack of investment, the acquisition of English as a new language—and diagnosing the underlying problem will be an important precursor to teaching into it.	When an opinion piece (or any piece of writing, really) is full of spelling mistakes, it can be hard for readers to understand what you are trying to say. Today, I want to remind you that writers try out multiple ways to spell a word before settling on one. Then, if they are still stuck, they consult a friend, writing partner, word wall, or other classroom resource.	Writers work hard at their spelling. They: 1. Try multiple versions of a word in the margin. 2. Pick the one that looks right. 3. Consult a peer, word wall, or other resource to help.
The writer struggles with comma usage. This writer is attempting to form more complex sentences but is struggling with the process. It may be that she uses commas incorrectly, interspersing them throughout the piece with little rhyme or reason, or that she simply doesn't use commas at all, resulting in long, difficult-to-read sentences. Either way, this writer needs help understanding the ways commas are used in sentences.	I've noticed that you've been trying to write longer, more complex sentences. Because of this, your writing sounds more like talking. It is quite beautiful. When writers write sentences that are more complex, though, they often need to use commas. Commas help readers know where to pause and help the sentence make sense. Today, I want to teach you a few important ways that writers use commas. Writers use commas in lists, to separate two or more adjectives, before (and sometimes after) names of people, and to separate two strong clauses that are also separated by a conjunction.	Use Commas To separate items in a list: • I want pears, apples, and oranges. To separate adjectives: • He drove by in his red, shiny car. Before and after names of people: • My brother, Peter, is a good friend. • John, don't be so silly! To separate two strong clauses that are separated by a conjunction: • I am working hard, but she is resting on the couch. • She is taking an afternoon nap, and then we will go out for dinner.

If ...	After acknowledging what the child is doing well, you might say ...	Leave the writer with ...
The Process of Generating Ideas		
The writer struggles to generate meaningful topics worth exploring. This writer feels stuck and has difficulty generating ideas for writing. Sometimes this manifests through avoidance behaviors (going to the bathroom, sharpening pencils), and other times the child simply seems to be in a constant state of "thinking," not writing. This child needs help not only with generating ideas, but also with learning to independently use a repertoire of strategies when stuck.	I've noticed that coming up with ideas has been hard for you and that you've had to spend a lot of time thinking about what to write. When you write opinion pieces, you want them to be persuasive. And for them to be persuasive, you have to *care* a lot about the topic! It can help to think about what you really care the most about—think about things you love or hate ... and then see if you can write opinion pieces about that.	Write what you love, write what you hate. Not in between.
The writer is exploring opinions that are overly simple or without dimension. This writer's notebook is full of entries about topics that are safe and relatively one-sided. If writing about his own life, he may be writing about how he loves his brother or how candy is the best treat. When writing about texts, the writer is apt to pick simple, obvious points to argue. Based on the work you see this child doing on a regular basis, you are sure that he is capable of developing more complex theses—those that take into account various points of view or that argue claims that are more difficult to prove.	You have been writing about clear, concise opinions like "Dogs make the best pets" and "My mom is my best friend." Today, I want to show you how to raise the level of the thinking work you are doing by raising the level of your thesis. One way to do this is by picking an issue that people have different opinions on. You can write first to explore one side of the argument, and then write to explore the other side.	Writers make their ideas more complex by exploring issues with multiple sides. "On the one hand, people think ..." "On the other hand, people think ..."
The Process of Drafting		
The writer has a clear plan for her writing but loses focus and organization when drafting. This writer seemed to have a clear structural plan for her writing. She went into the process with folders full of evidence or neatly sorted booklets. But, as she began drafting, all this organization seemed to fly out the window. That is to say, this writer put pen to paper and wrote, wrote, wrote—leaving behind any thoughts of groupings and paragraphs.	As opinion writers, it is important to make an argument in a clear, organized way. This allows the reader to follow what you are saying point by point. To create an organized argument, opinion writers make sure they rely on the plans they've created. It often helps to draft each part of your essay on a separate piece of paper, dedicating a new sheet to each reason. Then, when you are finished, you paste it all together.	Writers Don't Leave Their Plans Behind! One way to make sure your drafts stay organized is to draft each section of your essay on a separate sheet of paper. Use a new sheet for each reason, and then paste the pages together at the end.

If ...	After acknowledging what the child is doing well, you might say ...	Leave the writer with ...
The Process of Revision		
The writer has a limited repertoire of revision strategies. This writer lives off of each day's minilesson. He is task-oriented and generally applies (or attempts to apply) what you teach each day. This writer may work hard to revise, but when asked what else he might work on, he struggles to answer the question. This student is living on your day-to-day teaching as if it is all he has, rather than drawing on a large repertoire of known writing techniques and strategies.	As a writer, it is important that you take control of your own writing life. Writers use all they know about revision to make their pieces stronger. One way writers push themselves to get even stronger at writing is by studying mentor texts. They look at texts that resemble the kind they hope to create, find places that seem powerful and convincing, and then ask themselves, "What has the writer done to make these parts so powerful and convincing?" Then they try out the same in their own writing.	Writers study mentor authors to help them revise. They: 1. Study a piece that resembles the kind they hope to create. 2. Find places that seem powerful and convincing. 3. Ask, "What has the writer done to make these parts so powerful and convincing?" 4. Try the same in their own writing.
The Process of Editing		
The writer edits "on the run," investing little time or effort in the process. This writer is not applying what she knows about spelling, grammar, and punctuation while writing. It may be that you have taught a particular spelling pattern, and she mastered it in isolation but is not using that knowledge during writing workshop. She may also spell word wall words incorrectly or other words that are known (or easily referenced). There is often a sense that the writer does not care about the editing process, viewing it as a cursory last step before publication.	One thing I'm noticing is that editing goes awfully quickly for you and that many times you skip over mistakes. I've even seen you misspell a few words that are right up here on our word wall! Today, I want to teach you that editing is a multistep process and something that writers have to take seriously. One way to focus all your attention on editing is to pick one lens first—let's say ending punctuation—and read through your piece looking *only* for places where you need to add ending punctuation. Then you pick a second thing to look for, like checking to make sure your use of *to*, *two*, and *too* is correct. And again, you read through looking for only those mistakes. Writers do this until they've made it through the entire editing checklist.	Writers take each item on the editing checklist *one by one*. Editing checklist: • Read, asking, "Will this make sense to a stranger?" • Check the punctuation. • Do your words look like they are spelled correctly?